Praise for *Brilliant NLP*

Drawing on their years of expert NLP coaching and training David and Pat have created a great, easy-to-read introductory book for newcomers to NLP. The real beauty of this book is that it can also be used as a toolkit for people with experience of NLP. Pat and David's straightforward explanations of NLP tools and techniques, skilfully blended with practical examples of how to use these across a range of scenarios (both personal and business), is a breath of fresh air amongst other more traditional, overly complex books on the subject.

Moira Foster-Fitzgerald, Director of Organisational Change Management, SGS College

Brilliant NLP is a great practical toolkit for those that want to broaden and expand self-knowledge and take control of their success. David and Pat share powerful and accessible insights into how NLP can be a remarkable force for change both personally and professionally.

Lorraine Hartill, Head of People and Organisation Development, EMC

Brilliant NLP continues its progressive journey giving you, the reader, more tools and examples in understanding how to develop your life and your relationship with the 'Brilliant World' around you!

Martyn Lax, Managing Director, Panacea Selection Ltd.

David and Pat have taken their classic volume *Brilliant NLP* and made it sharper and brighter than ever. The earlier editions established their clear, practical approach, breaking down the barriers that some of us (as sceptics) initially had and making NLP a realistic tool for everyday use in business. This latest edition introduces new chapters to set NLP firmly in the business context, and a host of subtler changes including 'Brilliant Recaps' to anchor each chapter, and, of course, more Brilliant Examples to hook the book to our own reality maps. Full of great techniques and wise insight, *Brilliant NLP* will get you going as a practitioner and still be a great resource when you're a Master Practitioner.

Andy Evans, Business and Technical Director, JRA Aerospace

I have referred to this book often and can confirm how good it is for keeping in touch with the fundamentals of NLP in a very practical way. I'm really pleased to see the new material, such as the chapters on time and on reality maps. This book has certainly enhanced many aspects of my life, both personally and professionally – thank you David and Pat!

James Millard, Asia Pacific Business Manager, NDC Infrared

NLP

Manage your emotions, think clearly and enjoy life

third edition

David Molden and Pat Hutchinson

Harlow, England • London • New York • Boston • San Francisco • Toronto • Sydney • Auckland • Singapore • Hong Kong
Tokyo • Seoul • Taipei • New Delhi • Cape Town • São Paulo • Mexico City • Madrid • Amsterdam • Munich • Paris • Milan

PEARSON EDUCATION LIMITED

Edinburgh Gate
Harlow CM20 2JE
Tel: +44 (0)1279 623623
Fax: +44 (0)1279 431059
Website: www.pearson.com/uk

First edition published in 2006
Revised edition published 2008
Second edition published 2010
Third edition published 2012

Pearson Education is not responsible for the content of third-party internet
sites.

ISBN: 978-0-273-77873-8

British Library Cataloguing-in-Publication Data
A catalogue record for this book is available from the British Library

Library of Congress Cataloging-in-Publication Data
A catalog record for this book is available from the Library of Congress

10 9 8 7 6 5 4 3 2 1
16 15 14 13 12

Cartoon illustrations by Bill Piggins
Typeset in 10pt Plantin by 3
Printed and bound in Great Britain by Henry Ling Ltd, Dorchester, Dorset

About the auth

David Molden is a personal development trainer and coach. As an NLP trainer since 1995, he has many years of experience working with people from all walks of life, including entrepreneurs, managers, sports professionals and children, in their ongoing pursuit of personal success.

David has a zest for life and an unremitting sense of fun. He maintains a high level of fitness and mind–body balance by training in kung fu and t'ai chi and has an interest in ancient wisdom and its relevance to today's society.

David is a director at Quadrant 1 International, a training and development company. He has appeared on TV and radio and is the author of several other books, including *Managing with NLP*, *NLP Business Masterclass* and *Beat Your Goals* as well as co-author of *How to be Confident with NLP* and *The Brilliant NLP Workbook*. (All published by Prentice Hall.)

Pat Hutchinson has a rich background of experience as an entrepreneur and leader of sales and marketing teams. She is an NLP trainer and a director at Quadrant 1 International. Pat is also the author of *How to Sell with NLP* and co-author of *How to be Confident with NLP* and *The Brilliant NLP Workbook*. (All published by Prentice Hall.)

Pat's combination of leading-edge personal change skills with a sense of practicality makes learning and applying NLP easy and enjoyable. Her ability to focus and get straight to the heart of the matter makes her a highly sought-after trainer and coach.

She has an enviable record of results with both individuals and business groups.

Both David and Pat can be contacted at:
info@quadrant1.com

Contents

Acknowledgements

We would like to thank all the people who have helped and supported us in the writing of this book – friends, family and the publishing team at Pearson Education. There are many more who made this book possible – all the people mentioned in this book whose names we have changed and who have achieved such great things with NLP. Our intention is that you will join them by having wonderful experiences in your life through the power of NLP.

What is NLP and what can it do for me?

NLP can change your life. It is a remarkable force for change. We know this because we've seen it happen with many, many people over many years.

As a result of using NLP, we've seen people bring their dreams to life and make huge things happen – career and life crises solved, managers bringing about radical change in their companies, couples finding happiness after realising what is really important to them, teachers finding new ways to motivate children to learn, entrepreneurs operating at world-class levels, people changing the way they are perceived by others. In short, we've watched people use what they've learned to become more successful in everything they do. These people are the reason we know that NLP is *brilliant* – it has

> we've seen people bring their dreams to life and make huge things happen

given so many the tools and techniques that have enabled them to take huge strides forward in their personal and professional lives, and you can join them.

Simply put!

NLP is a set of tools and techniques to help you deal with unhelpful patterns of thought and behaviour (some you won't even know you have) and introduce new, positive and constructive ways to improve your life. Although there are many tools and techniques in NLP, you don't need to learn them all to get started and *gain immediate benefit*. You can make amazing changes by using just one technique – simply use the exercises to experience what NLP has to offer and prepare to be astounded by the results.

A bit of history

NLP was created by Dr Richard Bandler and Dr John Grinder in the early 1970s in California. Bandler and Grinder have long since gone their separate ways, but have continued to develop NLP models and techniques. In the last 30 years or so, many others have contributed to this evolving field of personal change – too many to mention here. Our more recent contribution can be found in the development of 'this not that' thinking in the section on reframing at the end of Chapter 4 and some of the exercises in Chapter 13.

Bandler and Grinder wanted to discover how successful people achieve their results and to then learn how to replicate their models. They began by modelling highly effective therapists and moved on to sales executives, negotiators, public speakers, trainers and leaders. Very soon they had drawn together the very best personal change tools from a variety of disciplines, plus models of excellence from their early subjects, and they designed the very first public training in NLP. Today NLP offers a vast array of effective tools and techniques for positive influence and change. Such tools have been used worldwide by literally millions of people to achieve significant results in all areas of personal and professional lives.

> NLP offers effective tools and techniques for positive influence and change

It does what it says on the tin

The letters 'NLP' stand for neurolinguistic programming. If you break down the name, it helps explain what it's all about:

- 'neuro' refers to the brain and nervous system
- 'linguistic' is the verbal and non-verbal language used to communicate
- 'programming' is the unique way you put all this together to create your behaviour.

You have one brain but two minds – one conscious and the other unconscious. When you get out of bed in the morning you begin running programmes stored in the depths of your unconscious mind – the one that remembers how to do all the things you do automatically: how to ride a bicycle, drive a car, make yourself feel good and make yourself feel bad. This storage area is much larger than the conscious mind you are using to read this book right now. The two minds work in a cooperative way – a typical example being when you are reading and your conscious mind suddenly switches to something else. Then, your unconscious mind takes over the reading and you arrive at the foot of the page not remembering anything about what you have just read.

brilliant example

When driving a car, the unconscious mind is capable of getting you from A to B while your conscious mind is focused elsewhere. You have probably experienced arriving home from work without remembering anything about the journey because you have been mulling over the events of the day. This works really well for you while events are ticking over normally and you can repeat habitual actions, such as changing gear, moving off when the lights go green, preparing to stop when they turn to red and so on. If, however, something untoward were to occur, such as someone pulling out in front of ▶

you, then your conscious mind would jump into action and take over. You then totally focus on the incident and all previous musing over the day's events vanishes.

Once formed, a programme has the capacity for amazing consistency, producing the same results over and over again. Some programmes will work well for you, while others may have undesirable results and be holding you back. NLP is used to change the programmes that are not working and create new ones that do.

brilliant example

Have you ever put your keys down somewhere and, then, five minutes later, forgotten where you put them? How can this happen? It's usually when you interrupt a well-rehearsed routine, such as leaving the house for work. You pick up your keys, grab your bag, check the back door, then, just before you open the front door to leave, you remember that you need to pick up some papers you really need. Now your conscious mind turns its attention to the papers and your unconscious knows you will need a hand to carry them so it instructs you to put your keys down. The trouble is your conscious mind hasn't registered *where* you put them down, so you have no visual memory of doing so. Interrupting deep-set habits like this causes all kinds of problems, but you can prevent them by being more consciously aware of your actions when interfering with an unconscious routine.

For most people, things happen and they react. NLP offers a better way. It gives you the tools to react differently by choice and be more aware of your thoughts, feelings and behaviour. You will discover what really makes you tick and begin to make crystal clear decisions about what you want from work and life. Only you can take responsibility for your results and make changes to improve the quality of your life. It's like taking firm hold of the steering wheel used to direct your career and personal life and driving it in the direction you want with a real sense of vision and determination. Once you have grasped it, you can use it to generate brilliant results in all areas of your life so you can not only find your keys or drive your car with greater care but also find work and relationships that are fulfilling and develop the strength and confidence to keep you in control of every area of your life.

How well do you know yourself?

Have you ever wondered how it is that two people facing the same set of circumstances can produce diametrically opposite results? Why do some people achieve infinitely more than others? You may also have noticed how some people have a tendency to attract lively, vibrant people, while others are very good at attracting moaners and groaners. There are people who seem to have life sorted out just the way they want it and others who are either just surviving or struggling with frequent problems and difficulties. So what makes the difference?

Successful people are often thought of as lucky, but is it really luck? Luck implies that there is some form of gambling involved but, on close inspection, these people show few signs of taking chances with their lives. Anyway, the sheer consistency with which they achieve good results defies the laws of gambling. No, it has more to do with **the way they think**.

Taking control of your thinking is key in the pursuit of success. To do this, you first need to realise the impact your thinking is having on your life. You may think that circumstances beyond your control are keeping you where you are, like a frog in a well who thinks that the small

> successful people are often thought of as lucky, but is it really luck?

circle of blue sky above is all there is outside the well. It is not until he clings to the bucket for the journey skywards that he realises how much more there is out there. The techniques used in NLP are designed to increase your awareness and, as a consequence, your choices in life.

Are you in or out of awareness?

Sometimes the patterns that work really well for you in some circumstances backfire in others, causing either you or others stress and frustration. These patterns have become so habitual that they exist outside of your personal awareness. Here are some examples.

brilliant example

Bernard believed himself to be a hardworking, focused, decisive businessman. He paid attention to detail and nothing escaped his attention. He revelled in his approach and believed that success was achieved through hard graft and strong leadership. He was totally unaware of the impact this was having on his most successful salesman, who felt micro-managed and undervalued.

brilliant example

Nagar fell in love with Said. He was attentive and caring whenever he was with her, but was often late when they had planned to do things together. Very soon they were making wedding plans and a family was on the way. What Nagar soon came to realise was that Said's attentive and caring behaviour took over whenever he was with his family, friends and colleagues. He was willing to do almost anything to help people out at the time they needed it. The more he did so, the more people asked of him and the less time he spent with Nagar and the new family.

New edition extras

We have received many e-mails from people who have read, enjoyed and benefited from the first two editions of *Brilliant NLP*. They told us how much the examples and exercises helped them to apply NLP personally, overcome what they thought were limitations and create more of what they wanted out of life. We continue to be delighted and often amazed at the achievements of our readers and so, in this new edition, we have included more brilliant examples and additional techniques in Chapter 13. All the examples used are real, but we have changed people's names to protect the confidentiality of those involved. We have also introduced a *brilliant recap* at the end of each chapter to help you integrate your learning. We trust that you will find the additional material useful and encourage you to e-mail us with your own examples of applying *Brilliant NLP* in your life.

Enjoy!

CHAPTER 1

How NLP gives you more choice in life and work

Think about a time when you felt really good about something you did and describe the feeling. What caused you to feel this way? How about the opposite feeling? Can you recall a time when you didn't feel so good about an experience? How well did you manage or cope with the situation? When you compare these scenarios, like most people, you realise that worthy achievements are driven by a sense of what's possible and a positive emotional state. Whether making money, passing an exam, learning a new skill or starting a new phase of life, feelings of confidence and achievement are strongest when driven by personal effort and passion.

Whichever way you look at it, we use imagination and positive states to feel good and drive us to achieve. In contrast, negative states hold you back by filling you with caution, anxiety, fear, uncertainty and insecurity. We are all capable of generating both negative and positive states. We are all capable of using our imagination to conjecture desirable futures and for seeing the worst that could possibly happen. We are all capable and we also all have choice.

How much choice do you really have?

Given that we have choice to think in whatever way we wish, some choose to focus on the downsides: what could go wrong; how this probably won't turn out OK. Others focus on the positives, imagining how things can work out well. Some people like to plan meticulously whilst others seem to live for each moment, preferring a more spontaneous lifestyle. Some people like to think deeply before acting whilst others are happier leaping into action without too much forethought. We exercise choice about what we do and how we do it many times throughout a typical day, but sometimes it may seem like we are not exercising choice at all because, over time, the choices we make become hard-to-shift habits.

So how much choice do you really have? Or perhaps a more apt question might be, 'How much of what you do each day is driven by habit, and which habits could you do without?' This is one area where NLP works magic, by taking habits that are not serving you well and re-programming them so you can be effective in more life and work situations. There's a popular myth that it takes at least 30 days to change a habit. Whilst this may be true by conventional methods, people have been using NLP techniques to change their strongest habits in a few days only, sometimes in less than an hour and in many cases just a few minutes. How is this possible?

The difference is in the 'How?'

When was the last time you questioned why you did something you were unhappy with? Maybe you flunked a test, had an argument with a colleague, got stressed about being late, presented poorly or acted inappropriately. Immediately after the situation, did you ask yourself why? This question might get to your core motivation for doing what you did but, if you want to change your habit, you need to be asking 'How?'

brilliant example

Joe's marriage had broken down and he got passed over for promotion twice at work. He began to feel the world was conspiring against him so he decided to start afresh.

He moved to a new town, found a new job and started all over. He immediately felt good having left behind all his problems, but, within a year, things were going off-track again. The same patterns were occurring. The future for his job was in question and he was dumped by a girlfriend he met six months previously.

Joe made the common mistake that many people make: blaming other people and situations for his misfortunes. This helped him feel better in the short term, but what Joe really needed was to look in the mirror for the things that he had been doing to sabotage his best efforts, to identify the habits that were causing the problem.

Joe's example reminds us that the changes we make on the inside help us to make the most of opportunities and challenges in the outside world. Joe eventually took an NLP Practitioner course and discovered how he had been re-creating his misfortune, initially by the way he had been thinking and acting towards others (including his ex-wife). He changed the way he perceived other people, learned to communicate more effectively and re-programmed some of the habits that used to get him into difficult situations. In essence, he used NLP to generate more choices to interact with the world differently. Joe is now settled in a loving relationship and has started his own business doing something he really enjoys.

What does this mean?

if what you are doing isn't working, try something else

There is a saying in NLP which you may have heard before, 'If what you are doing isn't working, try something else'. The 'something else' is ideally the 'difference that makes the difference', and often this is a very small change. You need to know what to change, and you get to this by reversing the thought process and learning about the way you have been relating to the outer world. For example, when you feel bad, how you made yourself feel bad is a typical NLP line of enquiry, as opposed to what you are feeling bad about, since your feelings are a result of how you have interpreted events in the outside world and are now representing them this way on the inside. Every time you infer a meaning or make a judgement you are exercising choice. The question is 'are the choices you are making getting you the results you want?'

brilliant example

Charlotte enjoyed her job as a sales executive selling IT services. She admired the top sales people when they won big seven-figure deals and aspired to be like them. The way to do this was to engage client directors, but Charlotte couldn't muster the confidence to approach them. She would come up with all kinds of silly excuses to procrastinate rather than pick up the phone to get an appointment. Her standard phrase to explain this dilemma was, 'I'm not a confident person'. Underlying this were all manner of limiting beliefs about directors either not being interested or being too busy, or that she may not be credible in male dominated boardrooms being a young blonde woman.

Charlotte became an NLP practitioner and, in the process, learned a variety of techniques to identify and change the limiting belief 'I'm not a confident person' that had been keeping confidence out of her reach. She rapidly grew her confidence and soon had a number of directors in her warm contacts list. This changed her results and, most importantly for Charlotte, she was able to realise her ambition as she saw the value of her commission cheques rise meteorically.

the first step in NLP training is to grow your awareness

We all live in the same world, but people perceive the world in different ways according to their experience and the influence of others. Many of your interpretations exist outside of awareness, so the first step in NLP training is to grow your awareness, and then you can make some simple yet profound positive changes that have a real impact on the outer world.

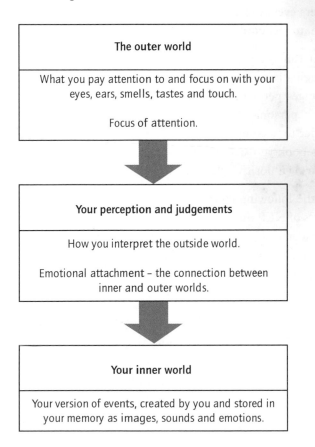

The outer world

What you pay attention to and focus on with your eyes, ears, smells, tastes and touch.

Focus of attention.

Your perception and judgements

How you interpret the outside world.

Emotional attachment – the connection between inner and outer worlds.

Your inner world

Your version of events, created by you and stored in your memory as images, sounds and emotions.

What am I capable of?

NLP is also good for stretching your capability to succeed in any endeavour. Our clients are testament to this: some have used their NLP skills to start new ventures later in life, others have secured high-level promotions. Our corporate clients are using their NLP skills to engage their employees, communicate effectively, coach executives and lead change initiatives. Many individuals have used their NLP skills to improve health, others to recover quickly from debilitating injuries and illnesses. Parents use their NLP skills to be the best parents ever, raising their children to be confident and cooperative individuals. NLP offers everyone a way to generate more choice, to be more flexible, to feel confident and to face the world on its terms.

You can get a glimpse of your fullest potential through your imagination, a central dynamic of NLP. One of the major changes people make after learning NLP is to raise the bar of their personal achievement. Suddenly things seem so much easier to accomplish than ever before. As you progress through this book you will learn how to use your imagination to create your own positive changes.

In the following chapters you will be introduced to the various parts of NLP that make up a wide and deep topic with a growing number of highly effective techniques to significantly enhance learning, communication and change. As you read the book, keep in mind something that you would like to change or you really want to achieve, and do the exercises with this thought in mind.

brilliant recap

In this chapter you have learned learned:

● how habits are created

● how you create your inner world by interpreting and judging outer-world events

● the connection between habits and choice

● the difference that makes the difference is in the 'How?'

● that NLP has many real-world applications

● how to use your imagination to make a positive impact on your results.

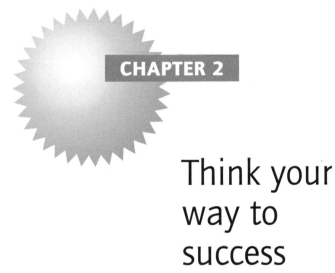

CHAPTER 2

Think your way to success

I magine your mind is like a kaleidoscope that has been left to form its own patterns over the years. Sometimes it falls one way and a pattern forms. Some time later, the kaleidoscope is knocked and it rolls into a different position, so the pattern changes and settles there for a while. Maybe this continues for a number of years until, one day, you decide to pick up the kaleidoscope and take control of the pattern making. With one small twist, the whole colour scheme changes and forms a completely new and more exciting pattern. Twist again and another one appears, and so on. The real challenge now is to decide which of the patterns is the most beautiful or, in terms of thought patterns, the most useful, empowering and enabling. So what is inside the kaleidoscope that makes up so many different patterns?

This chapter takes a close look at the driving force behind your behaviour, i.e. what you perceive to be important to you, your values. Your values are derived from a variety of sources: some imprinted from childhood from peers, parents, siblings and some selected from role models, heroes, teachers, friends. By the time you reach adulthood, your values are fairly well embedded into the unconscious part of your mind and there they remain until you take time to discover which ones are working well for you, whether some may require modifying or, indeed, whether some no longer serve any purpose at all.

What are you storing in your unconscious mind and how useful is it?

Your kaleidoscope patterns represent how you think about yourself and your experiences, including:

- values
  - what's important to you personally
  - the value you place on people, things, places, activities and information
  - your intrinsic values (also called metaprogrammes)
- beliefs
  - what you believe about yourself and others
  - your opinions, judgements and capacity for conjecture.

What is important to you?

What is really important in your life? How about your work? What is it about your work that makes all the effort you put in worthwhile? What's important about your relationships with your partner, your immediate and extended family, friends and colleagues?

When you ask these questions of yourself, where do your answers come from? Do they come from your head or your heart? These are your values – the things in life that are really important to you and that you will go out of your way to protect, uphold and defend.

So, do you know, with conviction, what is important to you? Does the tone of voice you use when you answer these questions match the words you choose to describe what is important or does it suggest that what you consider to be important to you is really an obligation? There is a big difference between a value borne out of obligation and one borne out of choice. This is a question you probably ask yourself rarely, yet the answer

provides an insight into why you may
be dissatisfied with certain areas of
your life. You may think that the way
to a fulfilled career and life is to set
goals, make a plan and get on with
it. If it were really that easy, wouldn't
everyone be doing it?

> while you are busy …
> the important things
> and people can get lost

Many of the things that are important to you are not even in
your conscious awareness. They are not so easily rationalised
and, while you are busy chasing a career, money, a partner, happiness or some kind of recognition, the important things and
people can get lost. What's important to you has a big impact
on the way you behave. So, if you feel that circumstances are
forcing you to do things that go against your values, then you
will feel an uncomfortable negative association, or tug, somewhere in your body. You may not know where it comes from,
what is causing it or even what it is about. Such tugs appear
in many different forms – it could be a feeling of discomfort,
a fleeting thought, an unpleasant memory or a shiver. The
chances are that you will ignore them and move on, but this
is your unconscious mind giving you a signal that something
demands your attention. You can
ignore it, but, if you continue to do
so, then you are suppressing the real
you and your inherent energy. When
energy becomes blocked, it can ultimately cause illness and disease. It
makes sense to pay attention to tugs.

> it makes sense to pay
> attention to tugs

Where do your values come from?

You will have gathered values all your life, starting from the day
you were born, and will have carried some of them with you into
adulthood. What are they? How did you get them? What influence are they having on you?

- **Inherited values** are possibly the most common. As a child you will have been influenced by what was important to your parents, siblings, extended family, teachers and group leaders. Later on you will have become a little more selective, adapting the values of your chosen heroes from the worlds of sport, fashion, film, music, politics, and so on. By the time you reached adulthood, your values were already forming a major part of your adult programmes. For example, if you were always told to finish your food at mealtimes, you may now be eating much more than you need. If your parents were very academic, you may put a high value on acquiring formal qualifications.

- **Compensatory values** are formed when you go to an opposite extreme to compensate for something that didn't happen for you. For example, if you had a deprived childhood, you may compensate for that by overindulging your own children.

- **Your own judgements** or the way you perceive your own experiences will have an impact on the value you place on them. If you have ever been burgled or robbed, you are likely to place a high value on security, which may not be appropriate in some circumstances.

On the surface, these values may seem innocent enough. On closer inspection, however, it is surprising what a major role they play in determining the way your life pans out. When you recognise an uncomfortable tug, a feeling that all is not well, examine your values to determine whether or not what you are doing is violating a deeply held value. Remember, you can choose to change your values or dispense with them altogether should you feel they no longer have a purpose. Use the following exercise to discover your true values and make choices that will serve you well.

Discover your true values

Step 1

Think back to a time when you last felt a tug. Was it to do with a relationship, your work, your family, your finances or your self-esteem and confidence? Then answer these questions.

- What is important to me about (the subject of your tug)?
- What else is important to me about (the subject of your tug)?

For example, you might start with 'What is important to me about my job?' and follow up with 'What else is important to me about my job?'

Continue asking this second question, making a list of your answers until you have all the possible answers. Then summarise the list and ask the question again. The thing *most* important to you may be so ingrained that you may not get to it until you have dug very deep indeed. You might list up to eight values, if not more.

In our example, you might get results such as, 'It's important that I am appreciated and valued at work', 'It's important that I am well paid' and 'It's important that my job has meaning – that it improves the world somehow'.

Step 2

Now, to find out what really is most important to you, take the value at the top of your list and compare it with each of the others in turn, asking, 'Which is more important?' Be firm and don't let yourself off the hook. Do this for each value in the list. You will end up with a hierarchy of values in relation to your chosen area.

Step 3

Now examine your top three values, one at a time, and form a view on whether what you are doing is expressing or violating these values. For example, if in your relationship with your children

▶

you place a high value on trust, but you find yourself checking where they are and what time they are coming home, then your behaviour is conflicting with your value. At this point you have a choice as to whether to keep the value and change the behaviour or vice versa. Other values will be driving some of your behaviour, so it is important to remember that the object of this exercise is to gain clarity about your true values and their connection with your behaviour as this will help you to make decisions that serve you well. The intention is not to determine your number one value.

If your values are being violated, what are you going to do about it? Can you change your behaviour to bring it into line with your values? Maybe one (or more) of your values is no longer valid and you have been hanging on to it as a result of habit. Where did it come from? Is it a value that works for you in some circumstances but not others? Can you change this value? Do you know someone with different values in this area? What would happen if you changed it? How would things be different for you? Asking these questions is the first step towards creating change.

> if your values are being violated, what are you going to do about it?

Intrinsic values

So far, we have looked at the values you have accumulated as a result of your life experiences. Underlying these are some deeper-rooted values that determine the way you approach life. Intrinsic values are easily recognisable because they show themselves as patterns in what you say, how you say it and what you do. The key here is not deciding whether the behaviour is right or wrong but whether it is useful in the circumstances or not.

We call these intrinsic values metaprogrammes and they are the source of your core motivation and behaviour patterns. Their impact on your own approach to life is described in full in the following paragraphs. As you read think also about people who may have the opposite pattern in each case and how this may affect the dynamics of your relationship.

Think of these programmes on a continuum, with 0 and 10 representing the extremes. You might function at one point on the continuum at work and at another in your personal life. There is no right or wrong – it is a question of whether or not it is useful in any given context. You will recognise yourself as we describe the extremes at each end of the continuum.

The towards and away from programmes

This pattern determines your most fundamental motivation. If you have a *towards* programme, you are recognisable by your drive. You set goals easily and are frequently creating new goals for yourself. Sometimes you disregard the risks involved and, at the extreme end, may not complete one goal before beginning another.

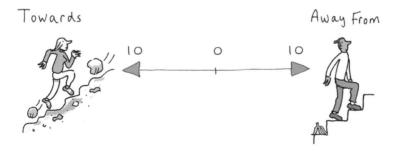

- Advantages – forward-thinking, goal-orientated, positive energy and drive.
- Disadvantages – may get entangled in too many new initiatives at once; may be perceived as gung-ho and have a tendency to leave things unfinished.

If you have an *away from* programme, you focus on avoiding risks and making sure everything is safe before moving forward. You sometimes miss out on life and work experiences as a result of fear of taking a risk. Typical behaviour includes being over-insured 'just in case' and, when asked what you want, replying with a list of things you don't want. You hold back from getting involved in anything new until all concerns have been fully addressed. You put a high priority on all forms of security.

- Advantages – very good at assessing risks and recognising what to avoid.

- Disadvantages – overly cautious, with a tendency to focus on the downside, may appear negative and unwilling to try new experiences and make choices based on avoidance rather than a desire for something new.

The options and procedures programmes

This pattern determines whether you operate from a position of choice or whether you prefer to follow a set procedure. If you have an *options* programme, you like to have choice in your life – considering different makes and models when buying a car, different areas when buying a house and the many varieties of food on offer when going out for a meal, for example. At the extreme end, your behaviour can be perceived as procrastination, particularly to someone who values procedure. You have a tendency to keep going over and over choices, as if making a decision might cause regret later.

- Advantages – explores many options and provides people with choices; happy to test and break rules.

- Disadvantages – may procrastinate and avoid making decisions until forced to do so by circumstances; very good at reinventing the wheel.

In a *procedures* programme, you have schemes to follow in order to be effective. You become confused and frustrated when faced with too many options. You write lists, tick things off as you go and are very efficient at completing tasks that require an ordered sequence. You may, however, find it difficult to accept a new procedure, which is more than likely to have been written by an options-orientated person. In order to get involved in a creative thinking session, you need a procedure detailing how to do it.

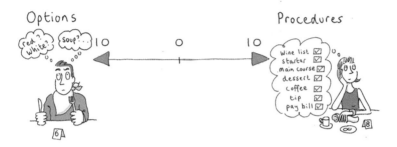

You require structure and clear processes for getting things done.

- Advantages – very efficient, good with rule-based administration and will stick to agreed rules.
- Disadvantages – the procedure may become more important than the job to be done; at worst, bureaucratic and blocking.

The in-time and thru-time programmes

How you code time will determine your approach to time-bound activities. You are *in-time* if you live 'in the moment', not worrying about what comes next – whether or not you are going to be late for your next meeting or arriving late at a party, if indeed you get there at all, for example. You give people your full attention because they are there with you now. You value each moment and are fully engaged with whatever you are doing at any one time.

- Advantages – can concentrate on tasks; emotionally and mentally engaged in each and every experience.
- Disadvantages – frequently late and can give the impression

of not being concerned about timekeeping; may get involved in too many things as a result of attachment.

If you spend your time planning and making sure that you are not late for meetings, parties and any other engagements, you have a *thru-time* pattern. This preoccupation with planning your next move or analysing the last may prevent you from concentrating on the matter in hand. Your thinking is constantly flitting across past, present and future. You may appear to others to be disinterested.

🔘 **brilliant** example

Eric is a training and development professional within the recruitment industry. Prior to learning about metaprogrammes, he didn't take kindly to people asking him at the beginning of a training programme what time it would finish. His answer was often terse, 'Bored already, are you?' Once he learnt about the *thru-time* pattern he changed his approach, understanding that the need to plan his timetable is important to a person with a predominantly thru-time pattern.

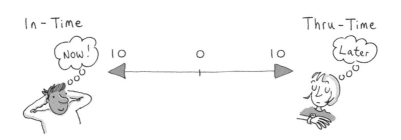

- Advantages – good planner and timekeeper.
- Disadvantages – may give the impression of not being engaged in the current activity; being on time and scheduling activities can become more important than the activities themselves.

The considering and doing programmes

This pattern determines the point at which you get started. With a strong *considering* pattern you will explore, and possibly research, all the implications of what you are about to do before you start. You will take into account the impact on all the stakeholders and environmental factors and weigh up the consequences.

- Advantages – when you do get going, your preparation will stand you in good stead: things can run smoothly and there will be few surprises.
- Disadvantages – in extreme cases, the need to consider everything can be time-consuming, particularly if combined with a need for options and choice. This may delay decision making and will, almost definitely, cause frustration to people at the other end of the continuum.

With a strong *doing* pattern the need to be active is very strong. Your preference will be to get going and deal with the consequences as you go.

- Advantages – you are perceived to be a person of action who can get things done; you will use phrases such as 'come on, let's get going'.
- Disadvantages – the road to success may be clunky as you deal with unforeseen challenges along the way.

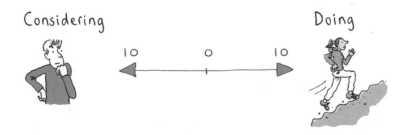

Considering   Doing

10   0   10

The internally and externally referenced programmes

The simplest way to think about our next pattern is in terms of how you measure yourself and how you evaluate situations. If you are *internally referenced,* you instinctively know when you have done a good job and will want to solve all your own problems. You rarely ask for advice from other people. You make decisions based on your own judgements, feelings and opinions. You don't need reassurance from other people. In fact, if you are given such reassurance, thanks or appreciation, you are likely to view it with suspicion. You will also know when you have done a job badly and this, again, will be judged against your own criteria rather than external evidence. You can appear aloof and insular and possibly overconfident to an externally referenced person.

● Advantages – can stay motivated when there is little feedback or praise.

● Disadvantages – internal standards may override, and sometimes cancel out, external evidence; will disregard evidence, facts and sound advice from other people.

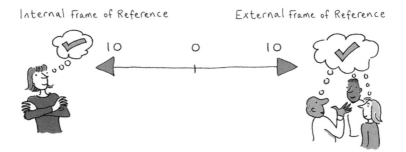

If you are *externally referenced,* you measure yourself against feedback from other people. You value this and will go out of your way to find it. To internally referenced people, you can appear needy and lacking in self-sufficiency. When faced with a challenge, you will seek facts, evidence, advice and opinions from other people and sources.

- Advantages – will make decisions based on concrete facts and evidence or maybe just the 'feel good' factor, so long as it comes from an external source; able to give excellent customer service and help to others.

- Disadvantages – will get stressed when there is a lack of external feedback; Needs frequent feedback on performance to make good progress; will be indecisive if there is a lack of feedback.

The self and others programmes

Who comes first – you or the team/family/group? If you have a *self* pattern, you speak in terms of 'I' and 'What's in it for me?' You believe that people are capable of looking after themselves. You help yourself to coffee, push in front of traffic queues, take the last chocolate and put yourself first when making decisions.

- Advantages – looks after self and is very self-sufficient; avoids getting tangled up in other people's problems.

- Disadvantages – does not engender good team spirit and sometimes may be perceived as arrogant and/or uncaring.

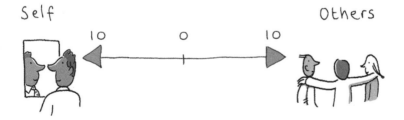

With an *others* pattern, you spend a lot of time making sure everyone is comfortable and happy, and may consequently neglect your own needs and wants. You serve other people coffee and put yourself last in the queue. You are a courteous driver and have a genuine concern for the well-being of others. Your day-to-day decisions are made taking account of other people, not wanting to cause them upset or discomfort.

- Advantages – good team player, looking out for the needs of others; does well in caring professions.
- Disadvantages – personal well-being can suffer as a result of putting other people first; can be perceived as unpredictable because many decisions are based on what others think and how they might react; considers the welfare of the team to be more important than getting the job done.

The detail and global programmes

These programmes determine the 'chunk' size of information you function with. As a person who enjoys *detail*, you will be concerned about the specifics of a situation. Your conversations are likely to be long and drawn out to cover all the details. Focusing on detail sometimes means that you forget the overall purpose.

- Advantages – very comfortable working with details and excellent at spotting small mistakes; copes very well with large documents and small print.
- Disadvantages – can get bogged down in detail and work away happily, even though the purpose may have changed; may be perceived as pedantic or fastidious.

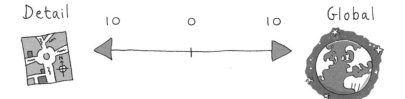

If you have a *global* pattern of thinking, you look at situations in terms of the bigger picture and speak in generalities, avoiding detail. You move conversations on to different topics in preference to discussing details. You may have little to say about some topics and may frequently need to be brought back to the point.

- Advantages – makes a good strategist or concept creator; can generate big ideas.

- Disadvantages – may appear to have your head in the clouds; may feel uncomfortable holding a detailed conversation; frustration with details may result in too many ideas and little execution.

brilliant example

Kim has an *options* and *global* pattern. She experienced feelings of inadequacy when her partner, who had a *detail* and *procedures* pattern, was able to book the family holiday efficiently, taking care of all the details. He would spend time studying brochures and, by a process of elimination, decide on the right one and book it, apparently without any feelings of stress. When Kim tried to do the same, she became distracted and overwhelmed by all the different choices. The reason for her frustration came from her preference for thinking *globally* and keeping her *options* open. Once she realised this, she was able to relax, laugh at herself and allow her partner to do what he is good at.

The feeling and thinking programmes

How do you convince people, through logic or feelings? With a *feeling* pattern, you react emotionally to a variety of situations and rely on your intuition or 'gut feeling' to make decisions. You are emotionally engaged with all life experiences.

- Advantages – can make good decisions based on gut feeling.

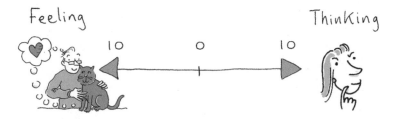

- Disadvantages – can appear emotional; others may be wary of evoking an emotional response.

As someone with a *thinking* pattern, you take a pragmatic and logical approach to situations while remaining emotionally detached.

- Advantages – decisions are made based on logic, fact and evaluation.

- Disadvantages – can appear to be cold and unfeeling; may not consider the feelings of others before speaking and acting.

The sameness and difference programmes

Do you relate to new experiences by looking for similarities or differences first? As someone with an extreme *sameness* pattern, you will probably visit the same place on holiday every year, take the same route to work each day, sit at your favourite spot in your favourite restaurant, eating the same food as you always do on the same night each week. When approaching something new, you will try to understand it by looking for similarities with previous experiences. Repetition doesn't bore you – it instils comfort and familiarity. You are likely to remain in the same job for many years.

- Advantages – can be relied on to complete repetitive activities successfully.

- Disadvantages – may be perceived as unadventurous by others; may not be willing to try new things, even if they could be beneficial.

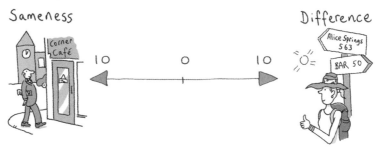

With an extreme *difference* pattern, you are likely to be constantly on the lookout for new things to do or new ways of doing current things. You rarely go back to the same place twice, always wanting to try new foods in new restaurants and new locations for holidays. You get bored easily and may find yourself changing jobs frequently due to a need for difference.

● Advantages – happy to try out new ideas and concepts; gains many different life experiences.

● Disadvantages – sometimes creates change for the sake of creating change; doesn't understand the concept of 'if it works, don't fix it'; lack of stability.

▶ brilliant example

Martin realised that he had a strong *difference* pattern and, every few months, he would become bored with his job and seek a change. Realising that this was not a recipe for success, he decided to accommodate his difference pattern within his role, and his social life, and was still able to progress successfully at work. When the tugs of familiarity occurred, he could recognise them quickly and deal with them.

The independent and cooperative programmes

How much personal space and control do you like? Someone with an *independent* programme will show this in two ways. Firstly, they like plenty of personal space wherever they are. When a space gets crowded, they may find a quiet corner somewhere they can occupy on their own. Physical personal space is valuable to them and they don't perform well in open-plan noisy environments. Secondly, they like to have complete control over their work and prefer not to share tasks with others. They feel it is easier to get on with things themselves with little input from others.

- Advantages – can work in physical isolation and be highly productive if not distracted.

- Disadvantages – frustration may set in where cooperation with others is needed; may lack social skills and find networking a chore.

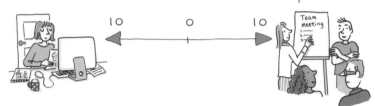

Independent   Cooperative

If you have a *cooperative* programme, you enjoy the company of others and enjoy frequent interaction with others at work. You like to be physically close to others and dislike being shut away to work on your own. Your own behaviour may be somewhat disruptive to independent types, but you need others around you to make work enjoyable. You are happy to share your tasks with others and like being part of a team.

- Advantages – you don't mind switching tasks and priorities when the team need your input and can work happily in bustling environments; active networker.

- Disadvantages – left unchecked your need for interaction with others could become a distraction to your work and other team members.

Metaprogramme combinations

Up to this point we have described each individual metaprogramme, but it is the overall profile that determines behaviour. A combination of metaprogrammes can either create extremes of behaviour or balance each other out.

Here are some particular combinations that could act as limitations or maybe benefits, depending on the context.

- **Options plus considering** – A recipe for procrastination, with so many options to weigh up and the process of considering each seemingly never-ending.

- **Options plus doing** – A perfect recipe for creative problem solving as the ability to create options is balanced by the need to get on with things.

- **Feeling plus away from** – This combination can cause stress and anxiety as negative thoughts create negative feelings.

- **Away from plus external reference** – This combination is likely to result in low self-esteem as the person focuses their attention on negative feedback and ignores or makes excuses for any positive comments.

- **In-time plus towards** – This combination can create a pattern of not completing things as there are always goals and targets to achieve, but a tendency to be distracted by the here and now.

- **Internal reference plus procedure plus detail** – This combination is often the driver behind perfectionists, who may say things like, 'This is the way to do it'; 'I am the only one who knows when it's good enough'; 'It is usually never good enough because there's so much detail to pay attention to and this causes me to be dissatisfied with most of the things I do.'

brilliant example

Tamara had been working as a supervisor at a high street store for many years. Every few weeks she would receive a product plan for her department, giving her directions as to how to lay out the products in the store. All stores were different and the plan was subject to variation ▶

according to space availability, shape and depth of shelves, and product availability. Tamara's store was particularly small compared with the others in the chain, so she regularly had to flex the plan, such that it didn't always resemble the diagram she was following. It didn't matter how often she was told by others that her display was excellent, if it didn't match the diagram, Tamara would not be satisfied and she would be constantly attending to details in an attempt to get closer to the plan.

- **Towards plus generalities** – Creating lots of goals and targets to achieve and talking about them at a high level in big picture terms is exciting, but getting down to the detail required for execution and completion can be a struggle. This may be perceived as blagging – another hair-brained idea that won't see the light of day.

- **Away from plus difference** – Repetition is a no-go for people who enjoy frequent difference and variety in their lives, but their 'away from' tendency causes them to choose new directions, jobs, relationships and habitats based on being dissatisfied with their lot rather than a desire for something they really know they want. They may become stressed when choosing their next change.

- **Away from plus sameness** – A recipe for a life which others may perceive as dull and dreary, as the need for security and repetition support each other and 'new' and 'different' don't enter the vocabulary.

- **Towards plus doing** – This is action man and bionic woman, never sitting still, always out and about doing things – can be exhausting to be around.

brilliant example

Ron was affectionately known as 'Action Man' by his friends and family. He worked as an operations director in a construction company, always coming up with new ideas and putting them into action. To others he appeared to have high levels of energy and found little time to sit still. When he arrived home, he would excitedly tell his family about his day over dinner and then take off to go to the gym or complete some project he had going in the garden or house. He appeared to need little sleep and rose early in the morning to get on with his day.

- **Others plus in-time** – A caring person, looking after people wherever and whenever they meet someone in need. They are great to be around, but can be frustrating when you are expecting something from them at a certain time and they are not around. You can feel let down as their attention is on other people they happen to be with.

- **Detail plus internal reference plus independent** – This is the micromanager profile, keeping your distance and only getting in close to pick someone up on a point of detail. Others may perceive it as untrusting and interfering.

- **Generalities plus away from** – This person can take a negative incident and generalise it across a wide range of contexts and scenarios. So, 'I had a tiff with my friend' becomes 'People don't like me'.

- **In-time plus self** – Can appear selfish as the thing that's most important in this pattern is 'What I am doing right now', and so a person with this pattern may not even notice the needs of others.

- **Independent plus internal reference plus thinking** – The comparative lack of feeling and extreme independent thinking can be perceived as arrogant. Feedback from others may be considered irrelevant.

- **Thinking plus procedures** – May appear robotic and inflexible with very little show of emotion, a little like Spock in the TV series *Star Trek*.

It is important to note here that descriptions such as 'robotic' and 'arrogant' are merely an interpretation of, or perception by, someone with an opposite pattern. Such interpretations may be far from reality, but it is the perception that will determine the response to a person's behaviour.

Using what you've learned about your programmes

By now, you will have an idea of your intrinsic values. With some, you will already have the flexibility to be able to operate at either end of the continuum. If you operate mainly from one end, you might reap the benefits in some situations, but you will also feel the effects of the disadvantages in others. With this book, you can develop flexibility over all the programmes, so you will have the advantages with none of the disadvantages.

> the mismatching of intrinsic values is a very common cause of misunderstanding, stress and conflict

The mismatching of intrinsic values is a very common cause of misunderstanding, stress and conflict in life. When people speak of a 'personality clash', it is invariably a mismatch of values or misunderstanding of metaprogrammes. For example, many relationships break down because of a mismatch of the in-time and thru-time programmes. As one partner is ready and waiting to set off to go out for a meal with friends, for example, the other is still chatting on the telephone, showing no sense of urgency. The thru-time person feels devalued and frustrated, while the in-time person wonders what all the fuss is about. It's the repetition and interplay of these patterns that eventually causes a relationship to break down.

Similarly, you can bore a global thinker rigid if you give too much detail about your journey to work or the state of your health or what little Suzie got up to in the bath last night.

Someone who places a high value on choice is going to feel frustrated if asked to follow a five-step plan, while a person who is always late and unprepared will irritate someone who values planning. Combinations of profiles can produce different behavioural patterns in different people. The mismatching of programmes in job profiles is a common cause of stress in the workplace.

These programmes are unconscious so, when you become involved in activities that go against them, you feel that uncomfortable tug. You may even say to yourself something like:

● 'Why am I always late for meetings?'

● 'Why is it that Sally and Paul always manage to book their holiday well in advance and I'm still messing around with the brochures while they are jetting off?'

● 'I hate my job, but I'll stay because I'm not sure if I would enjoy a new one.'

● 'Why do I never finish anything before I start something new?'

● 'I never seem to make up my mind to do anything.'

● 'It doesn't matter how hard I work, my manager never seems to appreciate me.'

Are your intrinsic values holding you back?

The examples given above demonstrate conflicts of intrinsic values, each having advantages and disadvantages. They indicate a lack of flexibility due to being 'stuck' at one end of a continuum. Here's an exercise to help you identify any patterns that may be the cause of conflict for you.

Identifying a conflict caused by an intrinsic value

Step 1

From the programme descriptions, choose those where you consider yourself to be predominantly at one end of the continuum concerned. Write the names of the programmes below.

Programme: _____

Programme: _____

Programme: _____

Step 2

Pick a situation where you have experienced conflict with another person or frustration with a task or responsibility.

Situation: _____

Step 3

Consider the role that you have been playing in this situation and ask yourself which of the programmes you identified in Step 1 is responsible for the conflict. Imagine how it might change if you were to function from the opposite end of the offending continuum. Take your time to think this through carefully. Acting so differently may feel awkward, but this is merely a sign that you have begun to develop your behavioural flexibility.

How you respond to experiences will depend on the nature of your values. If you once trusted someone and were let down, there are a number of ways in which you could respond. You may decide never to trust anyone again or you may decide that any future trust will have conditions attached. Alternatively, you may retain your belief in trusting and hope that one day this person will also realise that. Each of these reactions has a very different underpinning value that results from the meaning you have accrued from your life experiences.

Adapting your intrinsic values to give you more choice

An awareness of your intrinsic values is very often enough to create change. Sometimes, however, awareness is not enough and circumstances may suggest that a change in behaviour could be beneficial. As the majority of behaviour is habitual, the challenge lies in breaking the old habits and developing new ones by repetition.

▶ brilliant example

Gary had an away from and external reference pattern and had spent a good many years making decisions based on what he wanted to avoid (away from motivation). This, coupled with his external reference pattern, caused him to be very uncertain about his own choices. Gary chose his current job 15 years ago not because he wanted it, but to avoid the insecurity of being jobless. This one decision led him to spend 15 years in a job he dislikes, surviving by avoiding any situation that he found awkward or uncomfortable, including meetings with other managers.

Gary's very powerful habit of both avoiding difficult situations and not knowing how to make good decisions brought with it a great deal of stress. Having been given a little help to change the habit, he is now pursuing a more fulfilling and engaging endeavour and looking a good deal younger and healthier as a result.

If you have developed a strong habit of behaving in a certain way, it may seem very odd to begin acting the opposite way by, for example, introducing difference when you are not used to change. You may not know how to act differently and find the change awkward and unnatural. This in itself will create a tug for you – a feeling that something isn't right – and you may want to revert to your more usual behaviour. If this happens, remind yourself why you want to change and that the tug will diminish the more you repeat the new behaviour. Think of the tug as a signal that you are making a transition from old habits to new and this will help you to become more flexible as a person. An excellent technique for generating new behaviours to overcome those that result from metaprogramme imbalances is the new behaviour generator in Chapter 13.

brilliant tip

Listen to your language, particularly your use of words like 'must', 'should' and 'need'. Are these words limiting you in any way? Are the things you consider important really so important? What if you were to relax your own rules attached to must, should and need? What new possibilities might be created by dropping your insistence on having things a certain way?

Develop a new habit by means of repetition. The more often you act in a different way, the sooner the new habit will develop.

Observe someone you admire, noting the way they act, and adopt their approach. Notice what they do and listen to the language they use. This will save you from having to work it all out for yourself.

brilliant recap

In this chapter you have learned that:

- intrinsic values (metaprogrammes) have a significant impact on our approach to life and work; they impact our perspective in any scenario

- there is no right or wrong to metaprogrammes, just consequences – particularly with extremes; they can be changed with practice and the new-behaviour generator technique

- combinations of patterns can create different preferences and subsequent behaviours

- metaprogrammes are context driven and can vary between social and business life, for example

- metaprogrammes can be used effectively in the communication and influencing process to create understanding and trust in your relationships.

CHAPTER 3

Be careful what you believe!

n the last chapter you learnt that what is important to you drives the way you think and behave. In this chapter we will explore the importance of the beliefs you develop as a result of your values. Sometimes such beliefs are empowering and serve you well. Sometimes they can limit your achievement in a particular area. For example, if you value openness of communication but believe someone who has been frank about a particular project to be difficult and obstructive, then you may struggle to communicate effectively with this person. We will look at ways of reframing and changing your beliefs to engender more empowering results.

Your beliefs are connected to your values and are very personal. They form a significant part of the pattern in your personal kaleidoscope. If you value trust because you like to be trusted, you are likely to hold beliefs such as:

- people can be trusted
- there is no need for rules
- people can manage their own schedules and productivity
- my children will come home when they say they will.

If you place a low value on trust, because in the past you were let down in a big way, you are likely to believe the opposite:

- only fools trust others
- people are out to get me

- I have to watch what you are doing because you can't be trusted

- I have to phone my children when it's time for them to come home.

The beliefs expressed above probably came from experience and it's amazing how little you need to form a belief. How many times does Johnny have to be late home from school before Mum develops a habit of reminding him to come straight home because she has formed the belief that 'Johnny is always late home from school'? How many times do you have to be ignored by someone for you to formulate the belief that he or she is uncaring or arrogant?

We're not saying that all beliefs are wrong or inappropriate, but, rather, that it is good to test them to see if they are acting as a barrier or limitation. Once you have formed a belief, it can become self-fulfilling in that others behave in a way that is expected of them. For example, if Johnny believes that Mum anticipates him being late, then he will develop the habit. If you regularly tell Johnny that he is lazy, he will prove you right. Holding a limiting belief is like wearing blinkers – you see only what you expect to see and block out counter-evidence. Because your beliefs are personal, you will defend them and seek evidence to justify them. This is fine if the belief is positive, such as 'Johnny has potential that is worth developing', but consider the consequences of believing 'Johnny will never make the grade'.

it's amazing how little information you need to form a belief

Are you being held back by limiting beliefs?

So who is turning the kaleidoscope of your mind? Who is imposing their limiting beliefs on you? The people around you will undoubtedly have a hand in making small turns, changing your beliefs and having an impact on your behaviour.

brilliant example

A mother and daughter attended the same training course. About to embark on a physical activity, the mother turned to her daughter and said, 'You'll never be able to do that, you are uncoordinated.'

Fortunately, the facilitator overheard the comment and the girl was asked to walk across the room. She did so elegantly, proving that she was indeed coordinated. Imagine being continually told that you are uncoordinated. What kind of limitation would that put on you? How long is the list of activities that you would go out of your way to avoid?

Think back to your schooldays. How many things did you do poorly or drop out of because you believed that you couldn't do them? Did your teachers, parents or peers reinforce or help you to create any limiting beliefs? Take a few moments to think of all the things that you could have been doing now if you hadn't carried those limiting beliefs to the present day.

At work, how many people are being held back by the limiting beliefs of their managers? In our workshops, we find an astonishingly high number of people who have had this experience. Many managers don't delegate, encourage, stretch or even recognise superb performance in their people. One reason for this is their belief in their own capability as managers and another is their beliefs about the capabilities of others. Helping teams to develop positive beliefs and values about colleagues can dramatically change attitudes, which quickly cascade through the company, with subsequent improvement in performance. If you can identify and change a limiting belief, you can make huge strides forward.

> if you can identify and change a limiting belief, you can make huge strides forward

A single belief represents just a small part of the kaleidoscope pattern and is often itself part of a cluster of similar beliefs. In the extreme, a cluster of limiting beliefs can lead into a whole host of unpleasant areas, including phobias, blaming others, anger and low self-esteem. Being in control of your own kaleidoscope, therefore, is key to your success. The simple demonstration in our brilliant example created awareness for the daughter that completely changed her beliefs about what coordination means. She went on to complete the exercise and learned to juggle three balls in under ten minutes.

You can't see a belief or touch it. Beliefs have no physical form other than the activity in your mind, but we need them in order to survive and thrive. Beliefs are powerful. Even though you can't see one, you can observe the results of a belief very clearly. In the extreme, beliefs are fuel for both suicide bombers and peace activists – the power of belief being used in very different ways. What you believe has an impact on just about every aspect of your life. Some beliefs may have a positive effect, others may not.

In your everyday life, you are making decisions based on the beliefs you hold. You may not be aware of how you are doing this. Indeed, most people are not – they are just aware of making decisions. Some people create beliefs to give reasons for things when they go wrong. A person who tends to be defensive when faced with a problem he or she caused is likely to create a belief in order to justify his or her actions.

brilliant example

Mike and Wendy are young parents of a three-year-old boy, Nathan. Mike tends to become defensive when his decisions are questioned. One day Nathan was having a tantrum while Mike was trying to concentrate on some urgent work. All attempts to calm Nathan down failed and Mike's stress level rose to a point where he picked Nathan up and shook him. This made matters worse, as Nathan fell to the floor, screaming and banging his fists. Wendy was looking on and shouted for Mike to stop. Shortly after the incident, Wendy asked Mike how he could have done such a thing to Nathan. Mike replied, 'You have to discipline kids or they will never learn to behave.' Clearly Mike was using this belief to justify his behaviour and either Nathan's tantrums will continue or he might respond by suppressing his feelings as long as that belief remains intact.

Beliefs take many forms and we are good at disguising them. We are also very good at accepting a belief when we do recognise it. So, when a friend says, 'No point talking to my manager, he's the last one to notice my ambition', we are likely to let it go by unchallenged or, at best, offer some advice, having accepted the belief as valid.

Beliefs can be either limiting or empowering. Are yours serving you well? How can you recognise them and what can you do about them? Let's look at how to challenge limiting beliefs that may be hindering you.

brilliant example

A hard-working woman recently presented us with the belief 'You have to work to earn money'. It was attached to a value about having enough money for her family to be secure. It was also important for her to have an active social life and spend time with her family. However, she had developed the habit of working late and at weekends. She became increasingly unhappy.

When she realised that the belief was causing stress, she let go of it. She continued to enjoy her job as well as spending time going to concerts with friends and being with her family. Very quickly her new, and more powerful, belief became 'Enjoying time with friends will give me the fulfilment that I am seeking'. This attracted a whole new set of beliefs about what she was and wasn't going to do. The initial change to her work belief triggered a series of belief changes, much like a falling stack of cards.

How do you recognise a limiting belief?

This may seem like a simple change, but beliefs can be stubborn, defying the most rigorous logic. First, you need to know how to identify a limiting belief from what people say. A limiting belief is a simple statement that will usually begin with one of the following phrases:

- 'I can't ...'
- 'People should ...'
- 'They don't want ...'
- 'Everyone/no one thinks ...'

Here are a few classic examples:

- 'I can't maintain a long-term relationship.'
- 'People never listen to me.'
- 'He is easily distracted.'
- 'Learning a foreign language is difficult.'
- 'I'm no good at maths.'

Here's a simple belief-changing exercise you can do:

Shaking unhelpful beliefs

Whenever you hear yourself making the kinds of statements mentioned above, use this exercise. There are three steps to take to change an unhelpful belief.

Step 1

Shake its roots by challenging it. Answer the following questions:

- Have I always believed this?
- Where did this belief come from?
- Is the belief still valid?
- What evidence do I have to support the belief?
- Who do I know who holds an opposite belief?
- What evidence suggests that the belief is untrue?
- In what way is the belief absurd or ridiculous?

Step 2

Find an alternative, more empowering belief – brainstorm for beliefs that open up more possibilities. This is a matter of 'trying on' a variety of beliefs until you find one that fits. Make sure that your new belief is stated in the positive – for example, 'I can learn a foreign language and I am learning something new in each lesson.'

Step 3

Integrate the alternative belief. Imagine how things will be different and gauge how you feel about this change. Imagine yourself doing what you will be doing as a result. Imagine having a conversation holding your new belief. Is this motivating you? Does it feel good? If necessary, try on another belief and go through the same process. Then select the belief(s) that make you feel really good about yourself. Before finally committing to the new belief, consider how it might affect other people.

Congratulate yourself for having taken control of your kaleidoscope. You have rid yourself of a limiting belief and created another that is infinitely more powerful. Even better is that, over time, this new way of thinking will become a habit and you will generate empowering beliefs naturally.

brilliant tip

Think of your beliefs and values as a tree. The values form the stable trunk and the beliefs are the fruit. Sometimes the fruit is fresh and bright and nutritious, sometimes it rots and falls off the tree and is no longer appetising. Every now and again, it's worth giving the branches a good shake so that old and unwanted beliefs fall to the ground.

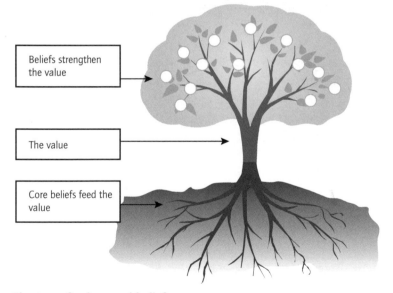

Beliefs strengthen the value

The value

Core beliefs feed the value

The tree of values and beliefs

brilliant recap

In this chapter you have learned that:

- beliefs can be empowering or limiting
- beliefs are closely linked to values
- beliefs are generally unconscious and linked to our neurological makeup
- beliefs dictate our behaviour as well as our physiological reactions
- beliefs can be changed more easily than values.

CHAPTER 4

Think your way to feeling great

Your mind will represent your thinking in pictures, sounds and feelings and sometimes even smells and tastes. The quality and detail of your representations will vary according to whether your thoughts are positive or negative. Knowing how you represent your thoughts, of which values, metaprogrammes and beliefs are a part, will help you make the changes you want in areas where you would like to improve your results.

When you feel anxious, uncertain, confused, angry or frustrated, you become tense and stressed. Being in that state prevents you from accessing all your wonderful inner resources. Whatever situation you are in, if you are feeling any of these, it is unlikely that you are performing to your full potential. Think of a time recently when you were feeling stressed and recall what was on your mind. Your thoughts were responsible for creating your feelings. Every thought you have results in a feeling, so the way to control your feelings is to control your thoughts.

Test this out. Sit quietly and think of a situation where you did something that you didn't feel so good about. Notice what feelings come up. Now take a deep breath and think about a situation where you did something that you felt really good about and, again, notice the feelings that come up.

> you can use the connection between your imagination and your feelings to put you in control

You have just used your imagination to recall two experiences that resulted in very different feelings. You can use the connection between your imagination and your feelings to put you in control and enable you to choose the way you feel. Your feelings have a direct impact on your capability, regardless of the situation.

It's the first thought that counts

Everything begins with a thought and that thought will attract similar ones until you have a cluster of thoughts. That cluster becomes a pattern of thinking, which forms a habit. The habit will then be applied to many different scenarios. Scientists believe that the conscious mind is able to cope with only about seven pieces of information at any one time and can become overloaded very quickly. This means that if you fill your conscious mind with negative thought patterns that create negative feelings, you have no room for anything else. By taking control, you are exercising more choice over your conscious thinking and, the more you do this, the more you will build a reserve of unconscious patterns that work effectively for you.

The first step in taking control is to be aware of how thoughts are generated. When you think, you have an internal selection process. If you were to absorb everything happening around you, your brain would become overloaded, so you select what you consider to be important and ignore the rest. For example, think about a conversation you had recently or a television programme you watched – how much of it do you remember? Chances are, you will be able to summarise the event and expand on the aspects of most interest to you, but you won't be able to recall every word. Your internal selection process has chosen what it wants to retain as a combination of images and sounds with the feelings you had at the time. Added to this will be some internal dialogue – in other words, what you have said to yourself about the situation.

This is how you represent your unique version of reality – in pictures, sounds, internal dialogue and feelings, as well as, sometimes, smell and taste. You capture your personal understanding of reality via a combination of your external senses and inner thoughts and it is this captured version that you use to make decisions and form judgements. This unique perspective of events is called your 'internal representation' or 'map of reality'.

Let's take a look at these components of your internal representation, beginning with the visual sense.

Working with your visual imagery

Bring to mind a pleasant memory and spend a few moments enjoying it. Capture the imagery, then come back to this page when you are ready.

Describe the image you created. Was it clear? Was it in colour? Did it have a frame around it or did the edges fade away? Did it have depth? Was there any movement? Was it bright or dark and murky? How about the contrast and detail? How close was this image to you and did you project it above or below the horizon? Could you see yourself in the image or was the image all around you?

Just as you can look at the visual details of a photograph or film, you can look at the details of the images that make up your thoughts. Those details refer to the qualities of the image, but not the image itself. The ability to imagine and change those qualities is unlimited. The number of different qualities you can work with in your mental imagery will be determined by the amount of practice you have had at doing so. Just as you intentionally imagined a pleasant experience, the very same process happens hundreds, if not thousands, of times each day to

the ability to imagine and change the qualities of your internal images is unlimited represent each thought you are having. Sometimes you may not be aware of your mental imagery, but it is there nonetheless and you can use it to good effect.

brilliant example

Harriet was having difficulty leaving her work behind at the end of the day. She was becoming more and more stressed as the pile just didn't seem to go down.

During coaching, we acknowledged that Harriet was very fond of pretty things. We asked her to visualise herself at the end of the day wrapping the outstanding work up in pretty coloured paper, tying a coloured bow around it and leaving it there until the next morning when she could unwrap it and continue with her work.

Harriet became much more relaxed about her work after that and her productivity increased.

Let's play around with your visual imagery a little and see how easy it is to change, or reprogramme, your thoughts and feelings.

Zap away bad feelings

It is quite easy to eliminate bad feelings for any situation in which you would like to feel more in control or be more confident.

Perhaps the thought of facing a difficult situation with someone is causing you to feel frustrated, tense or low in confidence. At times like these, when you are emotionally stressed, you consume a great deal of energy making yourself feel bad. Even though you don't enjoy feeling bad, it may be something over which you have had no control in the past. When you are feeling this way, you have entered the realm of 'self-preservation'. As a result, your ability to think rationally and make sound decisions is impaired. The goal then becomes one of survival, saving face, winning or seeking recognition. You only have to feel that way once or twice before a habit, or programme, is formed and then you have set a pattern for thinking yourself into bad feelings.

Eliminate the bad feelings by using the following technique:

Zapping away bad feelings

Bring to mind a specific time when you were unhappy with the way you felt or behaved.

Now focus on the image that comes to mind as you first access the memory. Quickly send it zooming away into the distance. As it goes, notice that it gets smaller and smaller until it disappears completely. It's just like the starship *Enterprise* whizzing off at warp factor 10 into deep space and, in a fraction of a second, disappearing completely from view.

You can do the same thing with all your images of unpleasant experiences – just zap them off into deep space. As you do, notice how much better you feel.

brilliant example

John had an away from pattern that was causing him a great deal of stress as he predicted all the awful things that might happen to him. He had plenty of time to dwell on his thoughts when walking his dog in the mornings. As he did so, his head would go down into the internal dialogue position as he told himself how awful things were.

During coaching, we suggested that, while out dog-walking, he might keep his head up and notice the scenery around him, visualising all the good things that had happened the day before.

Now exercise your ability to *choose* something *different* using the following technique.

Choosing to respond differently

As soon as you have zapped away the negative image using the technique described above, bring to mind a memory with positive feelings attached to it. It might be an experience where you were very confident or highly motivated to achieve a positive result.

Now work on the image. Make sure that it is colourful, big and bright.

When you have intensified those qualities, bring the image closer and imagine stepping into it. Take a few moments to absorb and enjoy the positive feelings generated by the effect.

Working with your internal audio

As well as making pictures in your mind, you can replay conversations with other people, environmental sounds and music. Do you sometimes replay conversations or anticipate a future event and actually hear what people said or might say? Your internal audio may or may not be accompanied by images.

> your internal voice is very powerful and has a direct influence on how you feel

What about your internal dialogue? What do you find yourself saying over and over in your mind?

Your internal voice is very powerful and has a direct influence on how you feel at any particular moment in time. A large part of how you feel is reflected in the tone of your voice – both your spoken words and those you say to yourself.

Here's something to think about. If you were to record all your internal dialogue for one day and then play it back, would it motivate you?

You can explore and change the qualities of your internal audio in much the same way that you changed your mental imagery above. Use the following technique to change the way you feel when you think about a future event. It can be used in all kinds of situations when you want to feel a certain way. How do you want to feel when you wake up in the morning, when you get to work on Monday, when your partner does something that annoys you? How many different voices can you create for yourself?

Use your inner voice to change the way you feel

Think about an upcoming event that is important to you and decide how you want to feel at that time. Now choose an actor or someone you know well who has the tone of voice that you want to have at the event.

Imagine that the event is just about to start and have a conversation with yourself in the tone of voice you have chosen. For example, you may want to feel confident and determined to get a result. Choose the voice of one of your heroes, saying, 'This is an important day for me. I will be asking some tough questions and expecting clear answers. I will be positive, focused and determined to get a result we can act on.' Now say it again and turn up the volume. Adjust the tone and pace until you begin to feel confident and determined.

You can also turn the volume down when your internal dialogue gets carried away with itself. When you keep repeating negative dialogue over and over, telling yourself what a mess you made of this or that or churning over a work problem when you are trying to sleep, simply turn the volume down and notice the words fading away into the distance until they have gone completely. You can

▶

also change negative voices into humorous voices, such as Bart
Simpson or Mickey Mouse. Notice how easily the negative feelings
disappear when you do that.

When you realise that you have control over your inner voice
and associated sounds, you can walk around with a symphony
orchestra in your head and a host of film stars and cartoons at
the ready, should you require their services. Have fun!

Feeling fantastic

The feelings you have during a day are the result of how you
have chosen to associate with your experiences. This is the
emotional domain. The word used to describe those feelings is
'kinaesthetic'.

Your feelings are generated by imagined events as well as real
experiences. If you have an argument with a partner or a disa-
greement with a shop assistant, the feelings you experience will
be part of a learned pattern of reacting to those circumstances.
A memory consists of visual, auditory and kinaesthetic elements,
sometimes including smells and tastes as well. Feelings result
from thinking in a particular way. For example, a feeling of
apprehension may be the result of creating dark, murky images
and internal dialogue that is warning you to be on the alert for
an awkward or difficult situation. Imagine how this contrasts
with the feelings of another person in the same situation who is
creating bright, clear images with internal dialogue that is full of
excitement.

You have the capacity for a wide range of feelings – from excited
highs to heavy lows and, at worst, depression. There are many
techniques to help you feel the way you want to feel. Some
of them help you to change the feelings you have attached to

negative memories, while others give you a way to create any feeling you want at any time.

Use your best experiences to feel great

The way we attach feelings to our thoughts is very haphazard. We allow people and circumstances to influence the way we feel. Once a thought has a feeling attached, it becomes well and truly anchored. Each time we recall that thought, the exact same feeling will surface. For example, when you look at a photograph taken on a great holiday, the feelings you had at the time return. When you answer the phone and hear the voice of someone you had a negative experience with, you feel the same way as when that experience happened.

Anchored feelings become embedded in your memory very easily. A classic anchor is when you have a bad encounter with a sales assistant and decide never to visit that shop again. Whenever someone mentions the shop's name, you relive the feelings you had at the time of your encounter, even though it may have taken place a long time ago.

The process of anchoring feelings to thoughts is an automatic feature of the unconscious mind. The result is called a 'state'. It is not just a state of mind but also a state of mind and body, as the way you think and feel causes the body to become either relaxed or tense.

Now, what if you could use this process to create great feelings, or states, whenever you wanted them? In other words, exercise choice over the feelings you anchor and the states you create. What if you could produce feelings of being courageous, confident, calm, decisive, optimistic, attentive, playful, empathetic, curious or focused? What if you could create a positive state for learning and being open-minded; for leadership, motherhood, fatherhood; for being dynamic or having abundant energy; for love, sensitivity? Well, you can with the following very simple technique.

brilliant example

Louise had to present to the board of directors on a regular basis. The more she did it, the more nervous she became.

On one particular day, she was excited that she was going to present her new idea, which would save the company a great deal of money. She was also anxious about blowing it and really wanted to get the board to listen to her idea.

We helped Louise to access a confident state she knew well from another situation and anchor this state to the boardroom door handle. As soon as she touched the handle, the confident state emerged and she was able to give her presentation.

Anchoring resourceful states

Decide which positive state you would like to anchor. Choose one from the list on the previous page – or you may have some other specific state in mind. For the purpose of this exercise, we will call it 'state X'. Read through the exercise and commit it to memory – you will need to keep your attention focused internally throughout the process, so you will not want to be checking the book for what to do next.

Preparing for the exercise

You are going to attach a state to a trigger point somewhere on your body, such as pinching your ear or squeezing your thumb. Choose something that you are unlikely to do accidentally and can repeat with precision.

The procedure

1   Recall a time when you had a strong feeling of having state X and keep thinking about that memory. Choose any context you like, as long as the feeling of state X is very strong. If you

can't think of one, then put yourself into an imaginary situation where you are in a high level of state X. Pay attention to the qualities of your image and any sounds. You are going to use your internal representation to intensify the feeling of state X. It may help to close your eyes as you do the exercise.

2   Project the image in front of you above the horizon level. Make sure you are looking at yourself in the image.

3   Put a frame around the image. Make it colourful and bright with a high level of contrast. If sound is involved, adjust an imaginary graphic equaliser so that it is across the full range of treble, middle and bass. Make it surround sound.

4   Intensify the colour, brightness, contrast and sound.

5   Slowly bring the image closer to you and notice how the frame eventually disappears until the image is so close it has enveloped you and is all around you. As the feeling of state X approaches the peak of its intensity, set your anchor by gently squeezing your thumb (or pinching your ear or whichever anchor you have chosen). Release the anchor as soon as the sensation begins to diminish.

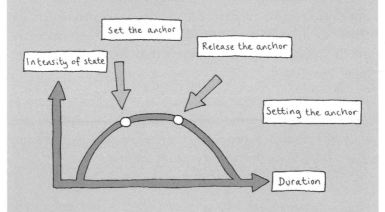

Setting the anchor

6   Now take a couple of deep breaths to change your state. Wait a few moments and then trigger or fire your anchor. Enjoy the intensity of feeling state X. Fire it a few more times to get used to it and strengthen it. Make sure that you break your state by breathing deeply between each firing. Now you can use this anchor any time you want to have the feelings associated with state X.

You can test the anchor by future pacing. Think about a situation in the future where you will want state X. As you run through the scenario in your mind, fire your anchor. The key to successful anchoring is the intensity of feeling, the timing of setting the anchor and the precision with which you set and fire the anchor.

Just as you can create a positive anchor, you can eliminate negative anchors. For example, you may have had a negative experience with someone when you did not cope well. You may have had bad experiences at work that are still causing you to lose confidence or become frustrated. Your reactions in those situations create a negative state that makes your inner resources inaccessible. Even though the incident might have happened some time ago, you still carry the feelings associated with it and behave accordingly. Your behaviour reinforces your state and forms a strong habit, such that, every time you find yourself in a similar situation, the limiting behaviour is triggered.

The following technique uses space and physical location to relieve those negative and stressful feelings. You needn't keep such bad feelings in your memory – you can collapse them and, if you wish, replace them with positive feelings.

brilliant example

Phil realised, with coaching, that he had deliberately been perpetuating a negative relationship with Sarah, his colleague. Whenever they met, he would be in a negative, defensive state, which Sarah would pick up on. They would argue and part feeling bad.

Using the collapsing anchors technique, below, Phil was able to establish a new way of approaching Sarah to rebuild the relationship.

Collapsing anchors

1 Mark two spaces on the floor about 2 metres (6 feet) apart.

2 Label one space with a minus sign, the other with a plus sign.

3 Stand on the minus sign and bring an unpleasant memory into your mind. Talk about the event for a minute or so and check how you feel as you recall the experience.

4 Take a couple of deep breaths and walk briskly over to the plus sign space, bringing a pleasant memory into your mind and make this more intense than the negative feeling. Talk about this experience for a minute or so, paying attention to the images and sounds you use to recall the events. Intensify the qualities of colour, size, clarity, brightness and volume, then bring the image close to you. Bring the image closer and closer and notice how your feelings intensify. Hold this feeling for a few moments and then relax.

5 Staying on the plus sign, talk again about the earlier unpleasant experience and notice how the negative feelings you had before have disappeared. You have collapsed the negative anchor.

Anchors in your environment

Anchors are all around you, causing you to feel a wide range of emotions – happy, sad, frightened, jubilant, angry or even nauseous. You may even be an anchor for someone else, causing them to respond towards you in a way that you may find confusing. Such responses can be either within your awareness, in which case you can connect precisely with the incident or circumstances that produced the feelings, or out of your awareness, in which case you can connect with the uncomfortable feelings but not the memories of the incident or circumstances that caused them. Here are some examples.

> anchors are all around you, causing you to feel a wide range of emotions

Meetings at work often highlight opposing viewpoints and sometimes emotions can run high. If not carefully managed, people can leave feeling negative and inadvertently anchor that state to any follow-up meetings on the same topic. This can have a number of outcomes.

brilliant example

As the sales director of a large company, Joe had been attending the same meeting on a regular basis, 40 miles from his home, for 2 years. The meeting always had the same format and people had adopted their own ways of dealing with the negativity that had grown over the years.

The meeting consisted of a series of reports from various sectors of the business. When he first started to attend the meeting, Joe had put forward an idea as a result of a presentation by the HR director, but his idea had been ignored. That caused Joe to feel that, if he were to offer ideas in the future, the same thing would probably happen. Because of that, the very thought of attending the meeting put him into a negative state. He never offered an idea again and, when others were speaking, Joe would be checking his e-mails on his mobile.

You could say that by checking his e-mails Joe was making the best use of his time in the meeting, if what he believed was really true. No one ever challenged him – they just accepted that was what Joe did in meetings, in the same way that Mary, the operations director, brought her production analysis sheets and worked on them until it was her time to present.

If no one was listening, what was the point of the presentations? Each director might just as well have produced a report and sent it round to their colleagues to read in their own time. The amount of high-level management time that was being wasted due to a set of anchors which had become engrained in the culture was extraordinary.

You need to prevent such anchors from taking root if high levels of productivity are to be maintained. Some simple steps would be to ensure that very clear outcomes for each attendee as well as for the items on the agenda are established, so individuals can make an assessment of the value of them attending the meeting. As far as possible, breaking routines, such as where people sit, the venue, length and format of the meeting, also helps to break negative anchors and keep proceedings fresh.

brilliant example

Chris was being coached. Following a number of personal relationship failures, he felt that he needed some help to restore his self-belief.

Things were going great until one day he arrived at the coach's house and tarmac was being laid outside in the driveway. The smell of the tarmac took Chris right back to a really nasty experience. The coach used the collapsing anchors technique to help Chris to regain his equilibrium.

Here are some everyday anchors that can evoke different states in people:

- music – a happy or sad song playing in the car, in the supermarket or on the television
- the smell of coffee, freshly baked bread, garlic or any other food
- the smell of vomit, hospitals, disinfectant, dog excrement
- the scent of perfume and aftershave
- a crucifix or any other religious sign – such signs can be strongly anchored in belief and evoke strong reactions in some people
- images of places, things and people
- negative notices in the working environment, such as 'do not move the furniture', 'keep out', and so on.

Advertisers know full well the power of anchoring – hence the use of music in shops to create a certain atmosphere, aromas to entice people into coffee shops and restaurants and the suggestion of wonderful relationships resulting from the scent of a particular aftershave in television advertising.

Once you are aware of what you are anchored to in your environment you can choose to change your responses. Take some time to notice things and people around you that trigger specific responses in you. If you enjoy a particular response and it is getting positive results for you, then use the anchoring technique mentioned earlier in this chapter to make it even more powerful. If not, then use the collapsing anchors technique to rid yourself of it.

You and others around you will slowly notice a change in you as you take control of your behaviour in response to triggers that may in the past have produced a negative response. Being aware of the anchors that trigger your responses, being able to change them and having the techniques to create brilliant new anchors gives you more control over your emotional states, your relationships and your life.

Fixing your phobias

Phobias are exaggerated anchored responses to everyday situations. They can cause muscle tension, hyperventilation, perspiration and dizziness. When a phobic response is being experienced, your internal dialogue and imagery will be predicting dire consequences. Phobias are irrational fears – as opposed to the rational fears caused by things that actually happen, such as the house being on fire. Because phobias are irrational, they are relatively easy to overcome.

NLP is very effective at fixing all kinds of phobias, including fear of bridges, confined spaces, open spaces, flying, lifts, spiders, bees, birds, frogs and snakes. This even extends to phobias about wet hair in the shower plughole, or oranges and bananas.

> NLP is very effective at fixing all kinds of phobias

In our experience, many people try to hide their phobias and avoid situations where they may have to face their fear. That is because they perceive their problem as being ridiculous and try to avoid the embarrassment caused by their reaction. At a deep level, this can have an adverse effect on self-esteem, as a phobia is often thought of as a weakness.

Underlying any phobia is a belief about what will happen in the situation causing the phobia. For example, when Paul was a teenager, he choked on an orange. Over time, he unconsciously anchored a negative response to that experience. Eventually, this became a phobic reaction to oranges, to such an extent that he had to leave the room whenever someone began to peel an orange. He believed that if he ate an orange he would choke.

The test for whether a person has a phobia or not – as opposed to being merely very concerned – is that he or she will react very physically to even the *thought* of the fear. Because it is the thought that produces the reaction, it can be eliminated without having to relive the experience.

If a phobia is affecting your enjoyment of life and/or your self-esteem, use the following technique – it has a very high success rate. We suggest that you familiarise yourself with the procedure before using it. This will enable you to complete the exercise without the distraction of referring to the notes.

brilliant example

During one of our programmes, Colin, a delegate, moved the curtains to shade us from the sun. As he did so, a large spider ran out and Colin virtually flew across the room and out of the door. Another delegate removed the spider and Colin returned to his seat, highly embarrassed. He explained the strength of his phobia and we suggested that, if he would like to deal with it, we could do so very quickly.

After a 10-minute phobia fix, Colin asked if he could go and find a spider. We found one in the conservatory and he was quite happy to stand and look at it from a distance of 6 cm (2½ inches).

Fast phobia fix

We are going to ask you to do a few things very quickly in your mind so that your phobia will never bother you again.

1   Imagine that you are sitting in a cinema and, on the screen, there is a black and white still picture in which you see yourself just before your last experience of having the phobic response.

2   Now imagine that you are floating out of your body and up

to the projection room, where you can see yourself sitting in the cinema. You can also see yourself in the still picture on the screen.

3 Turn the snapshot on the screen into a black and white film and watch it until just after the unpleasant phobic experience. When you get to the end, stop it as a still. Now jump inside the picture and run it backwards in colour. Everything in the film will happen in reverse – people walking backwards, talking backwards and the scenery moving backwards.

4 This completes the exercise. Take a few deep breaths and test the results by thinking about what it was that you used to be phobic about.

Reframing

The exercises in this chapter will have helped you to work with the emotions attached to your thinking and given you access to your inner resources. There may be times when the *way* you are thinking is creating a barrier. You can change your perspective completely by reframing this kind of thinking in a number of ways. In the same way that placing a new frame around a picture can give it a whole new appearance, placing a new frame around your thoughts can give you a very different perspective.

brilliant example

Frank was 'at his wits' end' (his words) regarding trying to get his youngest son, Timmy, to keep the house tidy. The relationship became increasingly strained as Frank continued to lay down the law. He often raised his voice and Timmy responded by retreating into silence and making himself scarce. The situation became progressively worse and Timmy's performance at school suffered. Frank explained that he was lost for a way to help Timmy

▶

'get his act together'. Timmy was getting a hard time from his dad and his falling marks at school were a direct result of stress.

We offered Frank the following reframe:

'It appears that you have been pushing Timmy to meet a certain standard of tidiness, which is causing him a good deal of stress and creating distance between you. His untidiness may, in fact, be a phase that kids of his age go through and a sign that he's behaving normally. By letting him be a normal teenager, you might find that Timmy is not so stressed and is better able to focus on his schoolwork.'

In short, Frank was offered a reframe that moved him from thinking 'my boy is untidy' to 'my boy is untidy, which is normal behaviour for any teenager'. It helped Frank to realise that his behaviour towards Timmy had caused the breakdown in the relationship between them. He immediately stopped hounding him about being untidy and started to help him more with his schoolwork.

This type of reframe changes the meaning of the situation. Another type of reframe shifts the meaning between contexts. For example, a person who may be highly critical of other people's ideas might be perceived by his team as being difficult or negative. The presence of a critic on the team can be very useful, however, when evaluating ideas resulting from a creative brainstorm. It's not that the behaviour of the critic is a problem, it's more a case of knowing how best to use that particular skill. This type of reframe puts the behaviour in a positive frame in another context.

A common cause of frustration in couples is demonstrated in the next example.

brilliant example

Fiona likes to be on time and is obsessive about dates, times, schedules and lists. Mike, Fiona's partner, is the exact opposite, preferring to take a more relaxed and laid-back approach to life. Mike was feeling torn, wanting to please Fiona while at the same time being unable to rationalise the pressure she was putting him under.

After some coaching, Mike realised that Fiona's ability as an organiser was useful in many ways, including remembering family birthdays, shopping, planning holidays and generally running the family very effectively. Having reframed his thinking in this way, the pressure eased. It was attached to the way he had been thinking, not to the circumstances.

Don't think that, think this!

Any reframe is simply saying, 'Don't think of it that way, think of it this way', 'It's not that, it's this!' You can apply simple reframes to all kinds of situations that are not working out as you would like.

A problem can only exist in your mind – outside your mind there are only sets of circumstances. That you call a circumstance a problem is indicative of your way of thinking. One person's problem is another's source of motivation. So, it really matters how you think about any situation you find yourself in because it has consequences.

> one person's problem is another's source of motivation

The words 'this' and 'that' are used many times during the course of a day, but, when used with tasks and people – for example '*that* task' or '*this* person' – they indicate whether the speaker is associated with or dissociated from what he or she is referring to. Where there is a positive intention towards a task/ person, there is likely to be a positive mindset around it – it's a *this*. When there is no positive intention towards it, there is likely to be a negative mindset around it – it's a *that*.

Being dissociated from something is a source of procrastination. If you could choose *not* to get involved, then there would be no issue, but, when you *have* to get involved because it's your job to do so, then you are *forced* to associate, which is when negative feelings can take hold of your thinking. In situations of forced association, it is useful to reframe your thinking and turn *that* into *this* with a positive intention.

There are four key principles involved:

1   You can be either *associated* (*this*) or *dissociated* (*that*) with tasks and people. When you are associated in a positive way, you are emotionally connected and likely to achieve better results than when you have put distance between yourself and the task or person, thus becoming dissociated. Poor performance results from 'forced association' with a *that* – when you perform a *that* task without a clear positive intention, you are forcing yourself to associate with it and so the emotional connection is likely to be negative. That is a recipe for poor performance.

2   Having a conscious positive intention prepares the way for success – all your intentions are positive for you, even though it may not appear that way to other people. Your unconscious mind may be telling you not to go ahead with an unpleasant task because its positive intention is to keep you feeling good. Having a clear positive intention and looking for the good in the task allows you to take control of your success. Just as a clear positive intention clears the way for success, so not having one causes you to struggle. Your unconscious intention will be to feel better and look for ways that mean you don't have to undertake

an unpleasant task or meet someone who makes you feel uncomfortable. In doing so, you cause yourself stress and discomfort.

3 When you exaggerate the absurdity of the way you are thinking about a situation, you prepare the ground for change. You can find absurdity in almost anything and use it to create change. An example demonstrating this follows in the next section.

4 Changing *that* to *this* is primarily a matter of focusing on what is good and having a positive intention. The concept of yin and yang demonstrates that, to achieve balance and flow in life, everything must contain an element of its opposite. Hot will contain elements of cold, good will contain elements of bad and vice versa. So, every *that* must contain an element of *this*. Unfortunately, while you are focusing on *that* you are oblivious to the *this*, which is undoubtedly present. Your results will be more successful if you choose to stay focused on *this* and allow it to develop and grow.

There can be any number of reasons behind you considering something or someone as a *that*. Examples of *that* could be:

● activities you don't enjoy and don't look forward to
● work that you don't feel fully competent to complete to a satisfactory standard
● someone or something you have negative beliefs about
● activities that conflict with a personal value
● someone you find difficult or frustrating to be with.

Using absurdity to create a change in thinking

You can find absurdity in just about anything. Consider the statement, 'I have to have dinner on the table by 6 p.m. every day.' It implies that all the family members will be hungry and ready to eat at exactly the same time every day. The likelihood of that being the case is remote and, therefore, the statement is absurd.

This technique takes the absurdity in your thinking and exaggerates it. In doing so, your situation becomes so ridiculous that you will want to change your view and reframe it because it is too painful to continue thinking in the old way.

brilliant example

Peter was a project manager who was a real stickler for detail and procedure. He had been given responsibility for a major project involving Simon. Simon became more and more anxious whenever he thought about the project.

Peter and Simon had clashed from the outset. Simon didn't know how to deal with Peter when he insisted on introducing details that Simon believed were unnecessary at the meetings. This began to affect his ability to contribute rationally. He would sneer and make derogatory comments about Peter's style of management in front of the project team. When questioned about the situation, Simon replied, 'He needs to learn a lesson if he's going to get on – I'll teach him, don't you worry.'

Simon was offered the following reframe:

'So, Simon, it seems you want to go on feeling bad about this relationship, don't you? You are going to continue to snipe at Peter and have everyone else laugh and snigger at you behind your back. You don't even mind that they perceive you as behaving like a child. The project will suffer and your emotional energy will be tied up in creating negative feelings towards Peter, so you will have very little left for creativity in relation to the project. You won't mind that, though, because teaching Peter a lesson is so much more important to you than building good relationships and getting the project completed successfully. Your antagonistic behaviour will serve you well when you find yourself not being invited on to the team for future projects. You may even find yourself without a role at all and that's OK because the most important thing here is to make Peter look silly, isn't it?'

This technique may appear a little harsh, but, with the right person, it could be the most effective tool to use. In this case, Simon is the type to allow his ego to get in the way, so the technique had to be stronger than his overinflated ego. What Simon received was a reframe that moved him from thinking 'Peter needs to be taught a lesson' to 'My career is more important than the way I feel about Peter'. This caused sufficient pain to Simon's ego for him to let go of the need to teach Peter a lesson and instead make positive adjustments to his own thinking and behaviour.

Focus on a positive intention

The absurdity technique may do the trick for some people (we hope you tried it out on your own situation with state X), but sometimes you may need a little more positive encouragement. However negatively you view a situation or a person, there is always some good to be found.

---

brilliant example

Michelle was having a problem with her flatmate, who seemed to be interfering in her life. She took it to mean that her flatmate didn't trust her to make her own decisions about boyfriends. Michelle began to mistrust her own judgement and became withdrawn, refusing invitations to nights out.

When questioned, she said that her flatmate didn't want her to have a good time and was jealous of her boyfriends. This frame of thinking caused a deep rift in the friendship.

Michelle was offered the following reframe:

'Michelle, could it be that your flatmate cares about you and doesn't want to see you get hurt? Maybe she has had a painful relationship and doesn't want you to experience the same pain. Perhaps focusing on the perceived jealousy is keeping you from noticing ways in which she really does care. However it may seem to you, the reality could be very different. If she does care for you, what is it she does that will tell you this?'

Michelle decided to look for evidence that her flatmate really did care about her well-being. She discovered lots of small things she did for her that had previously gone unnoticed. The relationship improved and they healed the rift. The point at which this situation turned around was when Michelle flipped her *that* mindset to a *this* mindset and created a positive intention to find the good in her flatmate.

Flipping a that to a this

1 Think of a task you really don't enjoy doing that causes you to procrastinate, or one you do very quickly to get it out of the way. Whichever you choose, it causes you bad feelings and, possibly, leads you to perform it below your usual standard.

2 Create a conscious positive intention relating to completing the task and begin to focus on the intention.

3 Either use the absurdity technique described above or begin to develop the positive aspects of the task, or both. How absurd is it that you have been thinking of the task in that way? Keep looking for the good and release your mind from the negative aspects of the task.

> thinking in a *this* way will allow your mind to be creative and come up with solutions and ideas

Thinking in a *this* way will allow your mind to be creative and come up with solutions and ideas rather than becoming stressed by the bad feelings associated with *that*-type thinking.

brilliant tip

Every new skill you attempt requires a degree of practice. The more you practise these techniques, the more you will reprogramme your thinking to create new feelings and behaviour that serve you well. Take one technique at a time and practise it several times on issues that are real for you before moving on to the next technique.

brilliant recap

In this chapter you have learned that:

- your feelings play a large part in who you are and how you behave – negative feelings produce negative results and vice versa

- you can choose the way you feel

- you can change your feelings using your internal imagery, dialogue and sounds

- changing your imagery and therefore your feelings will help to create better results

- associating with your images (*this*) will make them stronger; dissociating (*that*) will weaken them; you can choose whether or not to associate or dissociate with your images

- you can use reframing to change the way you are thinking about something

- phobias are the result of distorted beliefs and can be fixed.

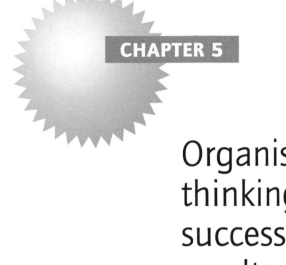

CHAPTER 5

Organise your thinking for successful results

So far we have focused on how one thought leads to another and how your thinking determines your behaviour. It's your behaviour that has an impact on the people around you and that they respond to.
Your attitude of mind is an important factor in forming your behaviour. So, if you have an aggressive attitude, your behaviour will take on aggres-

your attitude directly affects your behaviour

sive qualities; if you have an attitude of superiority, your body language will send that message to others; a relaxed attitude will result in a relaxed posture.

From this we can see that your attitude directly affects your behaviour and consists of a collection of experiences generalised into a set of values and a complex web of beliefs. In *Changing Belief Systems with NLP* (Meta Publications, 1990), Robert Dilts developed a universal model to explain how this works. You can use it to organise your thinking for successful results in any context. You first of all consider each of five levels of thinking in relation to any specific purpose, as shown in the diagram that follows. Awareness of these levels will make it easy to choose the most effective NLP technique for the change you wish to make. The key to using this model is to begin with a clearly defined purpose.

Alignment Model

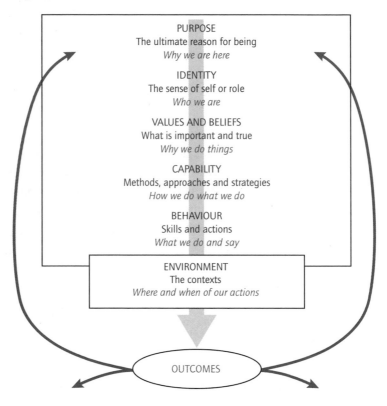

Is your purpose crystal clear?

In all situations, you have an intention. Often this is unconscious – that is, you engage with other people or undertake tasks
without first thinking what you intend to achieve. For example,
what is your intention when having a particular conversation
with your partner? Is it to inform, gain support, satisfy your
need to be heard, seek attention or something else? What is your
intention when undertaking a part-time job or choosing a new
career? Is it to leave behind a tedious or stressful job, do something you have aspired to for some time, increase your income
or have flexible working hours?

If your intention is unclear, then you run the risk of behaving in a way that will sabotage your best efforts and leave you feeling dissatisfied. A classic example of this is when someone is feeling bad about his or her life in some way and decides to move to a different city or country to make a fresh start. At a deep level, the intention is to remove the bad feelings that have grown over time. What often happens, though, is that the new life follows exactly the same pattern of events as the previous one.

Having a clear sense of purpose will enable you to make a conscious choice about how you approach situations. It will bring your deepest intentions to the surface and determine the role you play in the pursuit of your purpose. Having clarified your purpose, the next step is to organise your thinking within each of the five levels of alignment shown in the diagram.

1 What role are you playing?

In life, you play many different work, family and societal roles. You may split your time between being a parent, sibling, provider, chairperson, technician, leader, carer or any number of combinations of roles. What's important here is not the *label* for your role, but how you define it because your definition has an impact on your results. The manager who defines her role as taskmaster and organiser will elicit a very different response from her team than the manager who defines her role as people developer. Children of parents who define their role as protectors will grow up very differently from children whose parents define their role as nurturers. The teacher with the role of disciplinarian and controller will elicit very different results from another who defines her role as challenger and learning facilitator.

The role you define in the pursuit of your purpose will interact with your values and beliefs, which determine what you pay attention to and what you ignore.

2 What values and beliefs do you hold?

If you are a nurturing parent, you will probably have strong values relating to providing opportunities for life experiences for your children. A manager who believes in getting the best out of people will have strong values concerning trust and the potential of the team. A teacher creating a positive learning environment will value discovery, exploration and creativity.

These values will be supported by any number of beliefs. The nature of a belief causes you to focus on your values and proves the belief to be true. So, whatever you believe to be true, you will seek evidence to prove it and ignore evidence to the contrary. That is why it is so important to make

> it is so important to make sure your beliefs are empowering you

sure your beliefs are empowering you to achieve the results you desire. For example, a teacher with the belief that a child has a learning difficulty will continue to reinforce the difficulty. On the other hand, a teacher with the belief that the child has potential, and the challenge is to find a way to release it, will undoubtedly achieve better results.

3 Are you limiting your true capability?

Your values and beliefs have a direct impact on your capability. Quite simply, if you *believe* that you can, then you will find a way of doing so. If you believe that you *can't*, then you won't bother to look for a way. Empowering beliefs unlock capability and limiting beliefs act as a barrier.

Limiting beliefs stop you from putting effort into things. It's like the kaleidoscope is stuck in the same pattern and you have the power to change it, but refrain from doing so because you

> if you value something enough, you will generate a belief that it is possible to achieve it

are either unaware or unsure of the consequences. Eventually the pattern becomes dull and loses its excitement. Once you believe that it's not possible to change it, then you will find every excuse to make this true. It is very common for people to use illness as an excuse for continuing to believe that they can't achieve something. You only have to look around you to find many examples of people who have achieved great things, against the odds, due to the power of their belief.

Values and beliefs work together – if you value something enough, you will generate a belief that it is possible to achieve it and put your energy into finding a way.

▶ brilliant example

Sally opted out of a language exercise, saying that she was no good at English. She explained how her English teacher had encouraged her to pursue a career with numbers because her English was so poor. She followed this advice, took a job as a junior accountant and disliked it intensely. She left after three years to work as a shop assistant, from where her career developed.

On being quizzed about her current role, she revealed that she had been promoted to the customer services team, writing letters for the department – and really enjoys it. Sally also receives regular praise for the quality and creative nature of her letters. Despite this praise, however, she still maintained the belief that she was no good at English and developed the habit of withdrawing from any activities based on language. The acceptance of her teacher's belief limited Sally's natural ability in this area for many years.

---

4 Is your behaviour aligned with your thinking?

Your behaviour is a result of the way you have organised your thinking at each of the three levels above. Once Sally was able to change her belief about her capability in English, it opened up a whole new range of activities for her. She began writing short stories and articles and even attempted some poetry.

Some of your behaviour will be working well for you, other aspects will not. Once behaviour becomes a habit, it is almost undetectable by you – until someone points it out.

brilliant example

A group of elderly couples were walking arm in arm through a hotel lobby to dinner. One lady was limping and carefully holding on to her husband's arm. As she limped across the room, she suddenly realised that she had left her glass of wine at the bar and took off with a determined stride to retrieve it. She had forgotten to limp. The limp was not in her leg, it was in her mind.

Which parts of your behaviour are no longer of use to you? What tugs are you feeling? What would happen if you gave your kaleidoscope a small twist?

5 Are you having an impact on your environment?

The way you organise your thinking at the four levels above will determine the impact you have on your physical environment. Limiting beliefs and an unclear purpose create stress.

The blame for stress is often placed on external factors in the environment. That moves the focus away from the self and, in doing so, takes away the power of influence. With empowering beliefs and a strong sense of purpose, you are likely to take responsibility for changing your environment. Even unconsciously, you are likely to have a positive impact.

> people who change things believe that they can

Often you may believe that the environment is causing you some stress and feel emotionally tugged. The stronger the limiting beliefs about your capability, the more likely it is that you will recognise what is wrong in the world yet do nothing positive to create change. People who change things believe that they can.

The first step towards taking control is to identify the level at which a tug is taking place.

brilliant example

Jamie is of Middle Eastern origin and settled in the UK with his beautiful wife Anika. He was finding life hard – not getting along with his colleagues at work, his social circle was getting smaller and he felt increasingly isolated. He blamed the culture in the UK and felt unable to fit in. He decided that it was time to move back to his home country.

Anika explained to us that Jamie was exactly the same in his home country. She didn't want to move back and knew that his problem was nothing to do with country or culture. Jamie was merely shifting the responsibility for how he was feeling on to the culture and country. Anika knew that the real problem was Jamie's shyness.

Fortunately, it took only one coaching session with Jamie for him to become aware of his shyness pattern and learn some strategies for making friends and being a more confident person.

Are you aligned with your purpose?

Sometimes a change in behaviour does not follow a change in thinking. Have you ever been in a position where you have done something that you didn't want to do? Perhaps you did it to please someone and then felt that you had done yourself a disservice. Maybe you made a decision to lead a healthier lifestyle and take up running or yoga, but, when the time came to attend a class or go to the gym, you let yourself down and reverted to your regular unhealthy habit. It's at times like these that you feel the instinctive tug of misalignment.

have you ever ... done
something that you
didn't want to do?

In NLP, this state of misalignment, resulting in a behaviour that doesn't fit with the other levels, is called 'incongruence'. Deep inside you want to act a certain way, but, when the time comes, you resist the inner urge and maybe tell yourself, 'Not this time, maybe next time'. That is incongruence and it is not something success thrives on.

Success requires congruence, which means an alignment of all the levels – from purpose all the way through to behaviour. Only then can you affect your environment in the way that you really want. Creating such an alignment is the process of building self-confidence, as you then know that you have executed a change of mind and acted accordingly. Being able to recognise when you are being incongruent is the first step towards making your desired change happen.

The feeling of incongruence doesn't have to stem from a major life realisation – it can happen during the course of a business meeting or in a conversation with a partner. So, whatever you are doing, it pays to be able to recognise feelings of incongruence.

When you take a close look at the times when you are successful, chances are you also feel happy and confident. Sure, you can imagine all kinds of bad things happening if you choose to, but, when you are engaged in the act of doing something superbly well, you will be at your happiest. There is a saying, 'If you have to ask yourself if you are happy then you are probably not.' Happiness is a state of mind and you arrive at it by being congruent in your actions.

Happy people attract happy people

In the same way that similar thoughts congregate in clusters, so do people. If you feel depressed, you will attract depressed people and upbeat people will avoid you. If you gain the skills to help people improve their lives, those who need you will find you. If you decide to be unhappy, you will be. That's how life works – it will bring you what you express with your whole being. Cynical people keep each other company and strengthen their cynical attitude. The key message here is, what energy are you giving off and who and what are you attracting?

Your feelings of incongruence are likely to transmit signals that other people will perceive as confusing and unpredictable. As a consequence, they may judge you as being unreliable.

You hear people referring to others as being smug, with a chip on their shoulder, arrogant, brash, stand-offish, stuck up, cold fish. These are all interpretations of the way a person is communicating. They may be true, but, as soon as you have interpreted a person's behaviour, you have also chosen to relate to them with that judgement in your mind. The real truth lies beneath the behaviour in the kaleidoscope of their thinking. What is being picked up is a misalignment between levels – the result of the unconscious tugs referred to earlier. The key is to develop 'curiosity' about what is causing a person to behave in such a way, rather than interpret the behaviour you see. Then, you reduce your chances of falling into the trap of acting according to a misinterpretation and increase the likelihood that you will begin to understand the person and communicate effectively.

In our work, we meet all kinds of people. They come to us because they feel stuck with some aspect of their lives. We have worked with managers who are not making the progress they want with their team, life coaches who are struggling to make ends meet, couples who have lost the excitement in their lives, directors who are petrified at the thought of giving a presentation to the board, professionals who are snowed under with tasks, stressed and losing sleep, workers who are not meeting their employers' expectations of performance, people with obsessions, phobias, stress, anger, frustration, apathy and all kinds of behaviour patterns that are causing problems. We meet people from all walks of life who are limiting their potential to succeed and be brilliant in all kinds of situations.

The one thing all these people have in common is a feeling of incongruence when they think about the conflict they are living with. What they discover is how one frustration or problem is related to others, such as weight loss or gain, smoking, cluttered thinking, frequent illness, low self-esteem, being able to feel and patterns of broken relationships.

> even though you can create a smokescreen for your thinking, your body is not easily deceived

When you feel under stress due to personal difficulties, your mind has a wonderful capacity to put your problems behind a veil. Doing so allows you to have some stability and maintain the status quo of your life, but passion and energy also become masked behind the veil. Even though you can create a smokescreen for your thinking, your body is not easily deceived.

You can fool your mind but not your body

Your mind and body are part of the same energy system and interact with each other in response to external stimuli. When you are having a tough day and your mind is working flat out to meet deadlines, stress accumulates in your body – for example, you may become tense and your breathing erratic. Your body will react to whatever changes your mind goes through and vice versa.

> your body gives signals to other people ... that something is incongruent

Your body gives signals to other people, so, even though you may be able to create a smokescreen and veil your problems in your own mind, others will intuitively know that something is incongruent. The only way to deal with this is to remove the veil of your thinking and create a change.

One of the people Bandler and Grinder modelled in the early days of creating NLP was Virginia Satir, a highly effective family therapist. Virginia achieved very quick results by using a unique way to help individual family members become aware of their incongruent behaviour. The behaviour she identified in *Peoplemaking* (Science and Behaviour Books, 1972) is not exclusive to dysfunctional families. You only need to look around to see examples everywhere.

Satir categories

Virginia devised four categories of behaviour that she identified as being responsible for many family conflicts, and one that can be used to resolve conflict and bring people together.

Distracter

Distracters seek attention to compensate for their feelings of loneliness or inadequacy. The positive intention behind their behaviour is to protect them from facing up to things. Distracting behaviour includes removing a hair from your jacket lapel while you are talking, sabotaging a conversation by making a joke, interrupting a conversation, frequently changing the subject. There are many other types of distracting behaviour that people use to deflect attention from a subject that may be reminding them of their feelings of loneliness or inadequacy.

Distracter patterns are usually learned early in life when you are at your most vulnerable to what is happening around you. At the time, the pattern is like a coping strategy, but it can become a long-term habit. Luckily we know how to break habits.

---

brilliant example

Derek was a forthright person with lots of confidence and intelligence. He was a senior director with a retail company and was getting squeezed out by other directors because they said that he was 'far too arrogant'. He had ▶

developed a habit of kicking or throwing around any small items within his reach. It was as if he were releasing some negative energy as a response whenever he felt that he wasn't being listened to or acknowledged, as if to say, 'Hey, I'm here, can you watch me now.'

Derek was astounded at the number of years he had been holding on to this pattern and, after coaching, realised that it was no longer required. He was then able to relax and respond in a more mature way without needing to be the centre of attention.

Placater

The placater is out to please – talking in an ingratiating way, never disagreeing and always seeking approval. Feelings of an inability to cope alone create a martyr or 'yes man' (or woman!) A placater is often the first person to accept the blame when things go wrong.

---

brilliant example

Jenny just couldn't stop herself from saying 'Sorry' at the beginning of almost everything she said. It was such a habit, that it just popped out all the time - 'Sorry for asking, but …', 'Sorry, did you want to use this?' or 'Sorry, sorry, sorry, I didn't think to ask, I hope you're not upset, I'm ever so sorry.' Jenny would say sorry for entering a room, sorry for being in the way and sorry for watching the 'wrong' channel on television.

Blamer

Blamers find fault, never accepting responsibility themselves, always blaming someone or something else. They feel unsuccessful and lonely. They often suffer from high blood pressure and come across as aggressive and tyrannical. They will tell you what is wrong with things and whose fault it is and, in doing so, become powerless to do anything about it. By blaming external factors, they have absolved themselves of responsibility.

---

brilliant example

Damian had a set way of doing things. He appeared outspoken and stubborn to those who knew him. The combination of away from and procedural metaprogrammes caused him to 'know' the right way to do things and he would blame those who disagreed when things didn't go his way.

Computer

Computer-like behaviour is that which is very correct and proper, but displays no feeling. The voice is dry and monotone and the body often very still and precise in its movements, which are minimal, masking a feeling of vulnerability.

---

brilliant example

Jo had worked with computers for a long time. Her main means of communication was via e-mail and she became awkward when in the company of others. Consequently, she remained as still as possible, speaking only when spoken to and her movements were controlled and deliberate.

Leveller

This is the category to be in. Levellers have few threats to their self-esteem. Words, voice tone, body movements and facial expressions all give the same message. Levellers apologise for an action, not for existing. They have no need to blame, be subservient, retreat into computer behaviour or be constantly on the move. They are great communicators and have the ability to build bridges in relationships, heal impasses and build self-esteem.

The leveller's response is a real-time, congruent response. All the other responses are the result of negative internal feelings causing words and actions to be incongruent. It is very easy, under pressure, to respond to a situation with, 'It's not my fault' or 'I'm sorry, it's my fault again' or laugh inappropriately or show no emotion at all. These behaviours don't allow you to seek out rational solutions. The leveller's response is the most effective behaviour for solving problems creatively.

Levellers:

- look for solutions
- have a conscious, positive intention behind everything they do
- hold strong positive beliefs about themselves and others
- operate from strong personal values
- store positive mind images
- are flexible in their behaviour when communicating with others
- establish rapport before trying to influence.

brilliant example

Kieran was the chief executive of a pharmaceutical company. His team had a high level of respect for him due to his ability to be straight and honest with them. He was able to drive the business, admit when he made a mistake, recognise ideas and ability in others and have fun while keeping a cool head.

You can learn to adopt these attributes in the following chapters.

 **brilliant** tip

Be careful what you think – it can so easily become a self-fulfilling prophecy.

brilliant recap

In this chapter you have learned that:

● aligning your identity, values, beliefs, capability and behaviour with your purpose will have a positive impact on your presence, which will radiate into your environment

● creating change at one level will impact the levels below

● in terms of Virginia Satir, a fully aligned person may be compared with a leveller

● according to Virginia Satir, dysfunctional behaviour manifests itself in four ways, which she called – placater, distracter, computer and blamer.

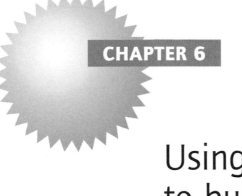

CHAPTER 6

Using rapport to build successful relationships

We all need people in our lives – to love us and for us to love, buy from and sell to, coach and be coached by, teach and learn from and enjoy life with. The results of your interactions with each individual you meet will be determined by your ability to get on with them, how much you are influenced by them and to what extent you influence their thinking and behaviour.

Whatever you do, your ability to influence others in all kinds of ways is important if you want to be more than a passive onlooker. Whether you are parenting, buying, selling, managing, leading, coaching, mentoring, relaxing or having fun, your degree of success in all these areas will come down to your ability to influence, and this requires skill in building rapport quickly.

> your ability to influence others is important if you want to be more than a passive onlooker

Think about times when other people have tried to influence you. Perhaps you have experienced a pushy sales assistant, a prescriptive boss or an overbearing partner. How did you feel at the time? Now think of a time when you were enticed by a sales assistant – what did he or she do that enticed you? Would you warm to someone whom you felt had no respect for you? Would you feel comfortable with a person who made no attempt to understand your needs? Probably not. Strong rapport is required to hold up a strong relationship – much like strong foundations will hold up a tall building.

Developing your ability to build rapport can help build confidence and contribute towards a more rewarding lifestyle with friends, colleagues and family. Rapport often develops naturally and you probably don't notice when it's happening. We expect you already have rapport with many people, but there will be occasions when a person who is important to your success is not on your wavelength and you will need to work at building a relationship with that person.

The role of respect in building rapport

In order to build rapport, you must first decide to respect the other person's perspective. How can you build rapport with someone if the outcome is uncertain or you don't feel confident in your role in that situation or you have a conflict of values? If you attempt to fake rapport, you will get caught out. People pick up your true motives and feelings from your body language and tone of voice, so, if you are insincere, it will show.

If you want to create rapport with someone, you must do it from a position of respect and a genuine need to understand them and seek win–win outcomes. When you feel congruent with your outcomes, identity, values and beliefs, then your behaviour will follow naturally.

Using what you do naturally – matching and mirroring

Have you ever watched two people deep in conversation? If they are both fully engaged in the exchange, they will unconsciously copy each other's body postures, movements, voice tone, pace and breathing. Sometimes they do it exactly – matching – and other times they are mirror images of each other – mirroring. It's like dancing to a rhythm.

You can use this knowledge and do it deliberately to provide the foundation for building rapport with anyone you choose. In NLP, as mentioned, it is called matching and mirroring.

Essentially, it works like this. People like people who are like them, so a sure way of building rapport with others is to be like them. You can build relationships and influence a wider variety of people by becoming consciously aware of what you do when you naturally have rapport. Equally, when rapport has been lost, you can take decisive action to rebuild it.

> people like people who are like them, so ... be like them

Using your body to build rapport

There is a common misconception about body language – that you can interpret what it means. If you base your approach to people on your interpretation of their body language, you will get it wrong much of the time. Interpretation will not get you very far. It is more useful to use what you notice about a person's body language in the matching and mirroring process. So, crossed arms doesn't necessarily mean that somebody is closed – they could just be feeling comfortable that way. If you also fold your arms, you will be joining them in their 'dance' and they will feel comfortable with you. Knowing that people have a tendency to interpret body language and often get it wrong, however, means you need to be aware of your own as others are likely to be making judgements about you from your posture, gestures and tone of voice, too.

> there is a common misconception about body language – that you can interpret what it means

Matching and mirroring body language is a highly effective method of creating rapport. At first it may seem a little wooden, but, as you practise it and learn to do it naturally, no one notices. It becomes an unconscious process. To be proficient at it requires you to overcome any apprehensions you may have. It's like learning anything – practising it makes it easier to do. Things that you can usefully match include:

- culture – what behaviour is specific to the culture where you meet the person?
- physiology – body posture, position, movement, gestures (when you are talking), breathing
- voice – tone, speed, volume, pitch, timbre, rhythm
- language – key words
- metaprogrammes – intrinsic values or core motivation traits
- experience – common interests
- vak (visual, auditory and kinaesthetic) – how is the person processing? What patterns of visual, auditory or kinaesthetic processing are they using? (This aspect of communication is covered shortly in this chapter)
- values – what people hold as being true and important – after sufficient pacing you can use values to lead the person to your ideas.

Pacing and leading model

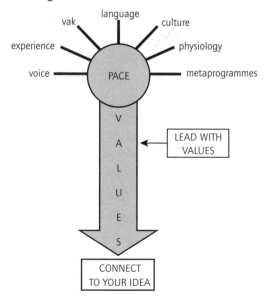

Matching and mirroring take place at the behavioural level. Think back to a time when you felt awkward building rapport and it just wasn't working, no matter what you tried. What was going on for you? Was it anything to do with the mirroring and matching or was it more to do with what was going on inside your head? Using the above list to match and mirror, how would you create rapport with a two-year-old child? How about a teenager? A pensioner? A particular person you want to influence at work?

How to match and mirror to create rapport

1 Think of someone you have not seen eye-to-eye with, where a better relationship would be good for you both. Imagine meeting that person.

2 Notice his or her posture and body language, then match or mirror it. You don't need total precision when matching. Are the arms folded? Is the breathing fast, slow, shallow or deep? Are the legs crossed? Notice the gestures used and use the same gestures when you are speaking. Raise or lower your voice tone and pace to match. Above all, be curious about what he or she has to say and acknowledge that you are listening. When you speak, use the same words as he or she does wherever possible rather than substituting your own preferred words - don't use 'shop' for their 'store'. This may seem unnatural, but it works. It is giving the other person a very strong message that you are a lot like him or her.

Time taken creating and building rapport will pay dividends in the influencing process. Be open and willing to be influenced by the other person's

lasting rapport requires sincerity and receptivity

perspectives. If you attempt to gain rapport and yet show no interest in understanding the other person, you are unlikely to succeed. Lasting rapport requires sincerity and receptivity – you need to really understand the other person's unique perspectives on how things are and not push yours on to them.

▶ **brilliant** example

Laura was struggling to understand her manager. Whenever she designed a complicated conference, she would present it to him and he would invariably ask about a small detail, such as what times the coffee breaks were. She felt that he was devaluing all the hard work she had put in, until we explained how his need for detail was driving his behaviour – it had nothing to do with Laura.

Next time Laura was in that situation, she simply pointed out the times of the coffee breaks and he was perfectly happy and didn't feel the need to check anything further. As a result, his trust in Laura's ability to attend to detail grew and so did the autonomy he gave her.   .

Pacing and leading

Having created rapport, you now have a foundation for influencing. Generally speaking, a person is unlikely to accept your views, opinions and goals unless they can form some attachment to them. Just telling a person what you want is not a smart option. First, make sure that you have strong rapport, then gently lead the person towards your thinking and create as much attachment for them as you can.

Pacing is the ongoing process of matching the other person's unique perception, thus strengthening rapport. The same applies in group meetings and presentations where you might begin by pacing common views or experiences. Once you have gained a good level of rapport by pacing, begin to lead and influence the other person or group. Check if the other person is willing to follow you by changing your physiology and noticing what happens. If you have rapport, he or she will follow you. If rapport is lost during leading, revert to pacing and regain rapport before continuing to lead to a desired outcome. The general view in NLP is that you need twice as much pacing as leading.

Taking the lead with your ideas

When you introduce a new topic to a conversation, unless the topic is popular, you risk breaking rapport. Why should anyone want to listen to what you have to say? Most people attempt to introduce their ideas into a conversation and justify them, as we all like to defend and protect what we consider to be important. A smarter way to have your ideas accepted is to connect them with the ideas already

minds like to be led to new ideas

held by the other person. You are then able to make a smooth transition to your topic. Minds like to be led to new ideas.

Some politicians are highly skilled at pacing and leading. Watch any interview conducted by a skilled television interviewer and notice just how such a politician manages to stay on track with what he or she has previously decided to talk about. Politicians without this skill tend to get bogged down in the details and cornered by the interviewer, and consequently become defensive and irritated. That is damaging to their public image.

Airtime is precious to any politician and the most effective ones know how to take control of it to get their message across, even when the topic in question is different from their message. First, they validate the concerns of the interviewer, then they skilfully use the technique of chunking, described below, to move back to their chosen topic despite the valiant efforts of the inter-viewer to draw them away. For example, 'This is a topic that is of utmost importance to our party and we will do whatever it takes to deliver a solution. Our party manifesto clearly outlines this issue, which duly depends on the priority we have set for stabilising the economy. This is our imperative and one that we are winning. In the last year we have seen the economy benefit from ...', and so on.

You can use this technique wherever you want to elegantly and subtly remain in control of the topic, such as when making a presentation, during a meeting where there are mixed opinions, in a debate or in any public speaking scenario. The next section explains how it's done.

People communicate using differently sized chunks of information along a continuum – detail and global being at each extreme. You can use this concept to pace and lead elegantly.

Here's a simple example of how information comes in chunks. Take the word 'tree'. A tree is part of a wood, which is vegetation, which is part of the ecosystem. So, here, we have 'chunked up' from tree to ecosystem. You can just as easily 'chunk down' from tree to oak to branch, to leaves. You can also move in a lateral direction from any level. For example, a lateral move from the word 'oak' would give us types of tree, such as birch, fir, pine, coconut, and so on. There are only three directions you can take during a conversation – up, down and lateral.

Here's how you might use chunking to gain financial support for a project.

You arrive at your manager's desk to find him deep in conversation about the latest cricket test match. You are not going to be very popular and probably won't get a result if you begin talking about money immediately. You need to find a way to lead him from 'test match' to 'financial support'.

In this example, there are seven levels, but, in reality, a conversation can range over any number of levels.

1 Corporate finance

2 Sponsorship   **Finance**

3 Professional sport

4 **Test match**   International football, golf, tennis, rugby

5 Teams and clubs   Australia, England, West Indies, Pakistan

6 Players   Umpires, spectators, organisers

7 Batsman   Bowler, fielder, wicketkeeper

From 'test match', you may choose to chunk up to professional sport, sponsorship and corporate finance or down to specific teams, the players and the roles they play. Here is how the conversation might go – notice how Kate joins the conversation at level 4 and takes it to level 2, from where she can naturally introduce her idea for sponsorship.

Peter (manager): Did you see any of the test cricket yesterday, Joe? (level 4)

Joe: Yes, isn't X playing well? (level 6)

Peter: I love test cricket. I find it relaxing and exciting at the same time. (level 4)

Kate (arriving): I saw the match yesterday, too. My partner is a cricket addict. (level 4) In fact, he is a sports fanatic full stop. (level 4)

Peter: Oh really? What other sports does he like? (level 4)

Kate: He is a member of the Y football club (level 5) and gets to see quite a few matches from the sponsor's lounge because he works for the Z software company. (level 5) It did really well last year due to a new product it introduced and sponsor Y is giving the club loads of publicity. (level 2) The club can't seem to do anything wrong at the moment.

Peter: Perhaps we should think about sponsoring a club? (level 1)

Kate: Perhaps when we have got this new marketing campaign off the ground it will give us the publicity we need to be able to approach a club. (level 1) I've actually got the figures here for you to look at, Peter. (level 2)

By working the levels in this way, you will be able to chunk to a level where you can cross over to your topic. In this case, the crossover was reached at level 2 when Peter mentioned sponsorship as it was then a simple step to the topic of finance. What you are doing in a strategy like this is joining in with the other person's value and staying with it, then linking that value in a subtle way with your topic. It's about facilitating a smooth transition from topic to topic.

Here are some more examples:

- Getting your young son from 'PlayStation' to 'room tidying'.

    You:　　What level are you on in your new game?

    Son:　　Level 6.

    You:　　What do you have to do to get to level 7?

    Son:　　Shoot all the aliens in the way.

    You:　　Wow, that'll tidy up all those aliens won't it? How many aliens are there in your bedroom?

    Son:　　Don't know.

    You:　　Shall we count them?

    Son:　　OK.

    You:　　Now, what shall we do with them to clear them out of the way?

- Getting your partner from 'football' to 'holidays'.

    You:　　　What's the score?

    Partner:　2–1 to United.

    You:　　　It looks really sunny where they are playing. Is it in this country?

Partner: No, it's in Barcelona.

You: Wouldn't you rather be there watching the match in all that glorious sunshine?

Partner: Of course I would.

You: Why don't we book a holiday in Spain and soak up some of that lovely sun?

● Getting your hypochondriac parent from 'What's wrong with me?' to 'Let's go out somewhere'.

Parent: I feel really ill today. I don't know what's wrong with me.

You: Really? What's been happening?

Parent: I keep getting dizzy spells when I get up out of my chair.

You: Dizzy spells? What are they like?

Parent: It's like having little stars in front of my eyes. They soon go away but it frightens me when it's happening.

You: Stars are really pretty. Why don't you try and capture them for a moment before they disappear? In fact, today I am going to take you to see lots of stars, including the biggest of them all – your granddaughter. We are going to the children's pantomime at the school. Come on, let's get ready.

You can have a lot of fun with pacing and leading as well as avoiding potentially confrontational situations. You will be surprised how easy it is to connect things in this way once you have practised the technique.

Fine-tune your senses for feedback

The communication process described above is greatly enhanced if you can learn to recognise the state changes discussed in the previous chapter in other people as well as in yourself. This means sharpening up your senses so that you can spot changes in yourself and others that usually go unnoticed. In NLP this is called 'sensory acuity'. Without good sensory acuity, the effectiveness of any techniques you learn will be very limited indeed. How can you have any influence if you are unable to read the way people are communicating and feeling? You may passionately explain to people how your master plan is brilliant, but, if they think otherwise and you miss their signals of disbelief, then you have only convinced yourself.

> without good sensory acuity, the effectiveness of any techniques you learn will be very limited

To influence others, you need your senses to be tuned in to certain physiological signs that indicate whether they are with you or not. If you miss the unconscious signals people transmit via their body language and tone of voice, then you are ignorant of most of the message they are conveying.

What you want to do is realise when a person's state has changed and whether or not the state he or she is in is useful for the outcome you have in mind. If you are selling, you want your customer to be in a 'buying' state. If you are giving a presentation, you want your audience to be in a 'receptive' state. For example, when we run workshops, we make sure that we pace and lead our participants from whatever state they are in when they arrive to a 'curious to learn' state before getting into the first session. We can only do this if we have the sensory acuity to identify their initial states.

It makes sense to prepare yourself, and others, before engaging in a matter involving communication or even when just relaxing.

> few people intentionally prepare their state for what they want to achieve

Surprisingly few people intentionally prepare their state for what they want to achieve. It is easy to end up in an inappropriate state for all kinds of activities – for example, going to seminars in a 'You can't teach me anything' state or 'Another boring seminar' state; going to work in a 'I hate Mondays' state or a 'I'm not looking forward to the meeting' state; arriving home after a long day's work in a 'Please don't ask me for anything' state or a 'The kids are making too much noise' state.

Here are some of the outward signs of a state to look and listen for:

- voice characteristics (tone, speed, timbre, volume, flow)
- body posture
- tension in certain parts of the body
- breathing pattern
- lip size
- pupil size
- lines on the face
- skin colour.

Assessing these external indicators of internal states is called 'calibrating' a state. Think of it as taking a reading of a person's state.

Noticing and recording states for future reference

When you meet a person who tells you that he or she is feeling frustrated, that is the time to calibrate the state he or she is in by assessing all the aspects of the person's physiology listed above. As the person is in a 'frustrated' state, you are unlikely to get him or her to connect with your topic while this state exists. If you ever have to deal with that person again, you will know what signs to look for that show he or she is frustrated. If, say, the signals are screwing up the face, squeezing the fists and grinding the teeth, if you notice these, you can begin to pace and lead the person into a more receptive state, rather than dive straight in with your idea and have it rejected simply because the person is in the wrong state to consider it properly.

Some people are not easy to calibrate – typically, those who like to keep their emotions to themselves. They will test your skills of sensory acuity and calibration to the full. Look carefully for changes in their physiology – maybe a very slight change in posture or lip size, for example. The signs will be there as the body always shows a change of state.

To develop your sensory acuity, you will need to practise calibrating the physiology of people as they change between states. Avoid trying to interpret what any state means. If you say 'Jack looks depressed' you may be correct, but, then again, you really don't know, unless Jack previously told you that he was depressed and his physiology at the time was the same as it is now. You can only truly interpret what a state means when the person has given you evidence that describes it.

Give people time to think

In any form of communication, people need time to think about what they are listening to and observing. They want to process information as it is received. While doing so, they have to stop listening – in NLP the term used for this is 'downtime'. Having the sensory acuity to notice when a person is processing in downtime is fundamental to building rapport, pacing and leading and, ultimately, effective communication. For example, during a conversation, if a person has his or her eyes open and directed your way, does it mean that the person is looking at you and listening? Could be, but, then again, if the eyes are glazed over or focused on a point somewhere in the distance, he or she is likely to be in downtime, thinking of something else.

The senses of sight and hearing can be directed either inwards or outwards. When you are 'in your head', running images, conversations and other sounds that make up your thoughts, you will not be taking in any information from around you, regardless of where your eyes are looking. In order to be fully alert to your surroundings, your senses must be focused outwards. When you are in conversation with another person, you know if he or she is listening to you from the eye movements – roving eyes or a distant focus tell you that other thoughts are uppermost inside the person's head.

Reading eye patterns for useful information

There are many aspects of physiology that give clues to how a person is thinking or feeling. One of the biggest giveaways is the movement of the eyes. Once you know what certain movements mean, you can determine how a person is accessing information and use this knowledge to influence them.

> one of the biggest giveaways is the movement of the eyes

The eyes are considered to be windows to the soul. They also indicate the way a person is thinking. Because the eyes are hard-wired to both sides of the brain, they move in accord with the thinking process. Unless you are a gifted mindreader, you still will not be able to tell *what* a person is thinking, but, with a little practice, you will be able to tell *how* a person is thinking.

A thought can consist of visual, auditory and kinaesthetic information, which is revealed by the position of the eyes. Just think for a moment how you can use this information with people you want to influence. If you can tell whether people are thinking in pictures, sounds or feelings, you can imagine how much more effectively you could communicate with them. Otherwise, the danger is that you miss the signals and totally mismatch modes of communication – for example, you use a 'feeling mode' with someone who is processing in a 'visual mode'. This is a common and frequent cause of miscommunication between people and, at worst, can create conflict. Depending in which direction the eyes are looking, you can pick up the mode the person is thinking in, as shown in the diagrams that follow, and avoid this problem.

Characteristics of communication modes

The following descriptions are valid for a right-handed person. Note that some left-handed people may be configured the opposite way around. While you read the descriptions below, keep in mind that we use all these modes of communication, but some people may rely on one dominant mode and use the other modes with far less frequency and clarity. Whichever mode is used most often, this will be the mode in which you are able to communicate most effectively.

Visual thinking mode

Upwards at any angle above the horizon is where the eyes go when you are accessing images. Up to the left indicates the recall of a visual memory and up to the right indicates a constructed image. Flicking from up-left to up-right and back again indicates that both recall and construction are taking place.

Visual recall

Visual construct

People who use the visual mode frequently in their communication often speak quickly and in a high pitch as they synchronise their voice with the images flashing through their minds. This process affects their breathing because, when you speak quickly, there isn't time to take in air all the way down to the lower abdomen, so you will notice the upper chest rising and falling.

In conversation, the visual communicator will have a tendency to choose visual words, such as:

- 'Can you *see* what I mean?'
- 'I'll *paint* you a *picture.*'
- 'It's *bright* and *clear.*'
- 'Let's *zoom in* on this.'

brilliant example

Tessa functioned at such a fast rate in the visual mode that she had 'forgotten' how to feel. She could see the solution to problems so quickly in her mind that she didn't stop to think about how she or anyone else felt about them. People had trouble keeping up with her and, consequently, her ability to communicate effectively was impaired. Over time, she had become severely stressed as a result and was having medical treatment for conditions that appeared to exist only in her mind.

On recognising this, and after some practice, she was able to reconnect with her feelings. She went on to make some major changes in her life and is now a much happier, healthier person.

Auditory thinking mode
A lateral left movement of the eyes indicates a remembered sound, such as a conversation or piece of music. A lateral right movement indicates a constructed sound or conversation. People who use the auditory mode frequently in their communication

Auditory recall

Auditory construct

tend to speak with a varying tone. They are likely to breathe from the mid-chest area.

In conversation, the auditory communicator will have a tendency to choose auditory words, such as:

- 'I *hear* what you say.'
- 'That *rings* a bell.'
- 'It *sounds* OK to me.'
- 'It's *music* to my ears.'

---

brilliant example

Paula lived with her elderly mother and was becoming increasingly frustrated about the amount of time her mother spent watching soaps on television. Paula functioned mainly via the auditory channel and couldn't understand the need for such visual stimulation. Paula, however, would go about her daily jobs with her personal stereo plugged in, listening to *The Archers*. Both were interested in soaps, but preferred different channels for them.

With her newfound awareness of this, Paula was able to be a great deal more tolerant of her mother.

Internal dialogue thinking mode

When the eyes are down to the left, it indicates that an inner conversation is going on. We all have an internal voice that we use to talk with ourselves as we are thinking or run habitual loops of dialogue.

There is no characteristic breathing pattern accompanying this mode, but it is common for people who are in deep conversation with themselves to put a hand on the side of their face or stroke their chin. This is the classic pose of 'the thinker'. You may even see the jaw moving, as if words are being mimed.

Internal dialogue

 **brilliant** example

Betty believed that she had a learning difficulty as she struggled to remember anything from lessons she attended. She had always thought that this was due to a lack of intelligence and poor memory.

During a training course, she learned that her internal dialogue was really to blame. Each time the trainer asked Betty a question, he noticed, from the position of her eyes, how she had been engaged in her own internal dialogue and, therefore, had not been listening to what was going on in the sessions.

On realising this, she made a conscious effort to stay tuned in to the trainer and, over time, managed to tame her inner dialogue.

Kinaesthetic thinking mode

Eyes down to the right indicate that someone is immersed in a feeling.

Kinaesthetic

A person in this mode is likely to be breathing from the lower abdomen area and speaking slowly, with gaps between the words. Sometimes the gaps will be long. The gaps are needed to allow time for feelings to form before committing a word or phrase to speech – it must feel right before it is said. The voice will be low-pitched.

In conversation, the kinaesthetic communicator will have a tendency to choose feeling words, such as:

● 'This just *feels* right.'

● 'Let's *run* with that idea for a while.'

● 'You had better *get your skates on.*'

● 'We're in for a *bumpy ride* over the next week or so.'

● 'Let's keep in *touch.*'

● 'I *get the hang* of this now.'

---

brilliant example

Graham used his feelings almost exclusively to communicate. During conversations he would take such a long time to form an answer that the person he was talking to would move the conversation on before he could ▶

finish a sentence. This led Graham to believe that people weren't interested in what he had to say. As a consequence, he developed the habit of tailing off his sentences before coming to the end. This reinforced his belief because people not only had to wait for him to reply but couldn't hear the full sentence when he did.

Once Graham realised this, he was able to finish his sentences with the same emphasis he started them and change his belief about people not being interested in him.

Using this knowledge to improve communication

Knowing the mode a person uses to communicate is very useful if you want to get on the same wavelength and make your communication as effortless and effective as possible.

Underlying this technique is the responsibility that *you* have for the communication process. Do not expect others to fit in with your style. Be flexible and adapt and you will have greater powers of influence. So, if you are asking someone a question using the visual mode, such as 'How do you see this panning out?' and the reply 'I don't see anything' comes back, it could be that you have chosen the wrong communication mode for that person. If, using your sensory acuity, you notice that the other person is using the kinaesthetic mode, you could then modify your question to fit with this, saying 'How does this feel to you as it begins to unfold?', for example.

> by modifying just a small aspect of your communication in this way, you can have a significant influence on people

By modifying just a small aspect of your communication in this way, you can have a significant influence on people. It's not so much the content of what you are saying that ensures you make the connection but the way you say it. Applying what you have learned about the visual, auditory,

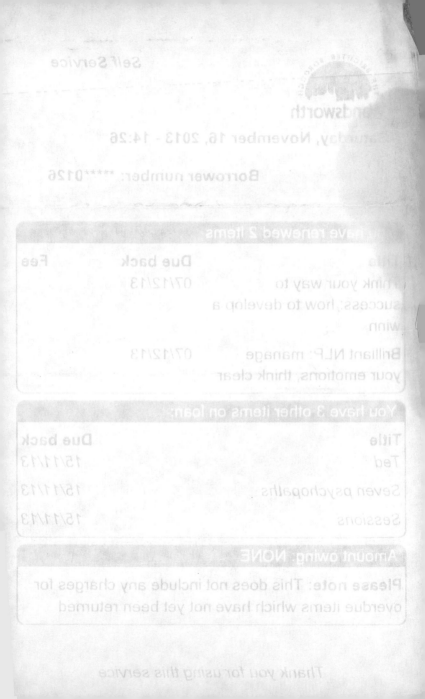

Self Service

Wandsworth

Saturday, November 16, 2013 - 14:26

Borrower number: *****0126

You have renewed 2 items

Title	Due back	Fee
Think your way to success: how to develop a winning	07/12/13	
Brilliant NLP: manage your emotions, think clear	07/12/13	

You have 3 other items on loan:

Title	Due back
Ted	15/11/13
Seven psychopaths	15/11/13
Sessions	15/11/13

Amount owing NONE

Please note: This does not include any charges for overdue items which have not yet been returned

Thank you for using this service

Self Service

Wandsworth

Saturday, November 16, 2013 - 14:26

Borrower number: *****0126

You have renewed 2 items

Title	Due back	Fee
Think your way to success: how to develop a winn	07/12/13	
Brilliant NLP: manage your emotions, think clear	07/12/13	

You have 3 other items on loan:

Title	Due back
Ted	*15/11/13*
Seven psychopaths	*15/11/13*
Sessions	*15/11/13*

Amount owing: NONE

Please note: This does not include any charges for overdue items which have not yet been returned

Thank you for using this service

internal dialogue and kinaesthetic modes of communication can have a big impact on how others respond to you.

brilliant tip

Building rapport is an elegant, sincere process. It can become very mechanical and obvious if you are not genuinely interested in the person with whom you are building rapport, so make sure that you use these techniques with integrity.

brilliant recap

In this chapter you have learned that:

- effective communication takes place once rapport has been built
- to build rapport you first need to pace and then lead
- the eyes indicate the way a person processes information and the direction in which they move can be used in the process of building rapport
- there are many techniques for building rapport through pacing and leading, including chunking, visual, auditory and kinaesthetic processing, values, beliefs, metaprogrammes, matching and mirroring body language, voice tone, pitch and pace
- as a general rule, you need to do twice as much pacing as leading
- rapport requires the respect of the other person's map of the world.

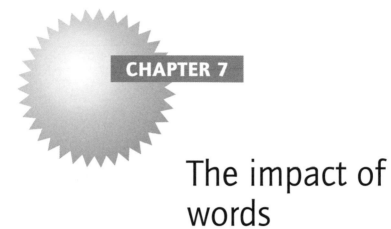

CHAPTER 7

The impact of words

I n the previous chapter you learned how to pace and lead using the concept of chunks of information and how words are an effective tool for creating change. Your language is just the surface expression of the structure of your experience, under which lies your kaleidoscope of values and beliefs, and the full real-world experience. In the same way that your thinking becomes habitual and forms unconscious patterns, so does your language. Your memory bank of language consists of stock phrases that you use repeatedly. These reinforce your thinking and a cycle is established. Is your language working for you or against you?

> is your language working for you or against you?

How to use high-level language for positive results

High-level language, or large-sized chunks of information, is vague. Consider the statement, 'kids nowadays don't care'. It is vague because it omits the details of which kids, which days, how they show they don't care and what they don't care about. A statement like this will have been formed as a result of the speaker applying his or her personal values and beliefs to experience. The danger is that the speaker will now seek further evidence to defend the statement and ignore anything to the contrary. Compare such a scenario with the same pattern used in a positive way – 'kids today are so creative', for example. Its vagueness begs the same questions as the previous statement, but the consequences are far more uplifting and empowering.

Both statements demonstrate the three ways in which the mind selects and attaches meaning to experiences for storing in the memory. The first is by *generalising*, as in 'kids'. The second is by *deleting*, as in how specifically they don't care or in what ways they are creative. The third way is by *distorting*, as in 'don't care' and 'so creative' – the observation being distorted to fit the perceptions of the speaker, to match what he or she has chosen to believe.

Milton Erickson was a highly effective and unconventional therapist. His methods were modelled by the originators of NLP in *Patterns of the Hypnotic Techniques of Milton H. Erickson, MD: Volume 1* and *Volume 2* by Richard Bandler and John Grinder (Metamorphous Press, 1996 and 1997). Milton used vague language to help people change the way they think. The language patterns he used became known as 'artfully vague' language. He used the patterns to help people change the way they represent their experiences internally, rather than give direct advice on what to do. Your personal perception of events is called your 'map of reality' and no two people's maps are alike. Reality maps are covered in Chapter 11.

Milton realised that his clients *wanted* to change, but making them defensive would not help. So, he agreed with whatever his clients presented as their map of reality, no matter how absurd it sounded. He then used language to make it easy for clients to create their own changes.

🔆 brilliant example

A sales executive wanted to improve his results, but was hesitant when talking to new prospects. The root of the hesitancy was an experience of a visit to a new prospect that didn't go well. The prospect ignored him and 'made him feel small' (his words). His memory of this event brought up the emotion of 'feeling small', which became a barrier to gaining new clients.

During the coaching he was questioned and offered statements that agreed with the way he was thinking. The manner in which the statements were delivered caused him to realise the absurdity of what he was doing to himself. One of the statements that created a big shift for him was, 'Wow! Isn't it incredible how you instinctively know that all new prospects are waiting for you to call on them so that they can make you feel small?' This statement agreed with his map of reality, yet emphasised the absurdity of it at the same time. There was nothing to defend or disagree with.

After coaching, he changed his perception of the negative experience, which allowed him to be confident about future visits to new prospects. As a result, his new client conversion rate increased significantly.

Think how often you use limiting language to yourself to determine what you can and can't do. Next time you hear yourself saying that you can't do something you would like to do, just

> think how often you use limiting language to yourself

listen to your reasoning and ask yourself where such 'beliefs' – because that's what they are – have come from.

Here are some language patterns to look out for. If you find yourself using them in a positive way, then generate more. The examples here demonstrate patterns being used in a limiting way and include questions that help to create positive change.

Generalisation

The speaker takes a particular experience and applies it to a multitude of other situations. Let's look at some examples:

'You can't run a family and work full-time'

- *Questions* What can you do? What stops you? What tells you that? Who can't? Do you know anyone who does? How many hours and days are you thinking of? What if you could?

- *Words to listen for* Can't, unable, not possible.

'Children need discipline'

- *Questions* Need? Which children? Discipline in what way? What else do they need? Who says?

- *Words to listen for* Need, must, have to, got to, necessary, requirement.

'Nobody loves me'

- *Questions* Nobody? Is there one person who does/doesn't? What tells you that? How are you measuring love? Do you love anyone?

- *Words to listen for* Everybody, nobody, anyone, every, always, never.

Deletion

Details are deleted as the speaker chooses what to focus on. Here are some examples:

'He's a failure'

- *Questions* How did he fail exactly? What did he fail at? Who says so? Has he failed at everything he's done? Is there nothing he has succeeded at? Has he not succeeded at drawing your attention? What else is he succeeding with?

- *Words to listen for* Instances where a verb has been turned into a noun, such as 'failing at' becomes 'failure' or 'he is performing' becomes 'his performance' or 'he is succeeding' becomes 'his success'.

'Her children are not very bright'

- *Questions* Compared to whom? What standard/who are you measuring them against? Bright in what way?
- *Words to listen for* Those that require an opposite, such as good, bad, cold, hot, bright, dull, sincere, insincere, happy, sad, rich, poor.

'She rejected me'

- *Questions* What did she do that you are calling rejection?
- *Words to listen for* Verbs that require clarification.

'They were left to fend for themselves'

- *Questions* Who are they? What do you mean by fend?
- *Words to listen for* Non-specific references to people/things such as they, people, computers, children.

Distortion

'He never buys me flowers so he doesn't love me'

- *Questions* In what way does him not buying you flowers mean that he doesn't love you? In what ways does he show that he loves you?
- *Words/patterns to listen for* Statements that don't 'add up', where a conclusion stated in the second part is based on the meaning attached in the first part.

'My children are driving me crazy'

- *Questions* What specifically are they doing to cause you to feel crazy? What are your children doing when you choose to go crazy?

- *Words and phrases to listen for* Statements in which one thing causes another.

'I know you don't want to support my initiative'

- *Questions* How do you know? What tells you that? You can read my mind?

- *Words and phrases to listen for* Statements that include conjecture and suggest mindreading.

'Families should stick together through all life's challenges'

- *Questions* Who said that? Who are you quoting?

- *Words and phrases to listen for* Statements that lack reference to the author.

Using what we've learned

NLP calls the above 'metamodel questions' because they make us aware of the higher-level (meta) meaning of our words. They bring into conscious awareness the deep-rooted patterns of meaning that have been created out of our values and beliefs. All too often, negative vague language becomes part of the programming we use in everyday life. You have seen how easy it is to develop beliefs that have a major impact on the way you behave. Your language is greatly influenced by your beliefs and associated values.

Artfully vague language patterns are positive and offer alternative choices in such a way that the individual is empowered to make whatever changes will help to bring about better-quality results. Think of the metamodel as an antidote to limiting vague language. It clarifies by getting to the specifics of an experience. It does this by questioning the generalisations, deletions and distortions that we have constructed.

When we break down language in this way, it's easy to see also how our thought patterns become demotivating and limiting – not only for ourselves but also for the people around us.

More insight into the way we use language can be gained from looking at the way we use the past, present and future tenses. You will often hear people say things such as:

- 'I will never be able to do that'
- 'I can't go under water'
- 'I'm not a team player'
- 'I don't seem able to hold down a job'
- 'I can't run for more than 10 minutes'
- 'My manager and I don't see eye to eye'
- 'I'm no good at numbers'
- 'If I tried that, I'd certainly fail'.

Note that all these statements are in the present tense – as a human being, you have an amazing capacity to carry past experiences with you in the here and now. Sometimes this is enjoyable – as when you recall pleasant memories and plan your future based on memorable experiences – but, when you apply the present tense to negative experiences, it can limit your potential. Your memories can be like old clothes. They become unfashionable or worn out, but you can't bear to throw them away, so they hang in the wardrobe, taking up space and preventing your other clothes from looking fresh and smart.

> when you apply the present tense to negative experiences, it can limit your potential

The problem with the makers of the statements above is that the desire to change is overshadowed by the strength of the belief they carry. By changing the tense of statements, you can start to gently loosen the hold of the limiting belief. Here are some examples:

- 'I will never be able to do that' *becomes* 'Up until now I have not been able to achieve this.' (Notice also the subtle change from 'that' and a flat dismissal of the action, suggesting dissociation, to the positive attempt at making it work.)

- 'I can't go under water' *becomes* 'In the past I have not felt comfortable going under water.'

- 'I'm not a team player' *becomes* 'My experience of working in teams to date has not been enjoyable.'

- 'I don't seem able to hold down a job' *becomes* 'Previously I have had some challenges settling into a job.'

- 'I can't run for more than 10 minutes' *becomes* 'I can run for up to 10 minutes.'

- 'My manager and I don't see eye to eye' *becomes* 'My manager and I have had one or two differences in the past.'

- 'I'm no good at numbers' *becomes* 'I have had a challenge or two with arithmetic.'

- 'If I tried that, I'd certainly fail' *becomes* 'I have never tried it before, but I am willing to have a go.'

The initial form of the last statement is interesting in that it is not even based on a past experience. It predicts failure and so prevents the speaker from even trying something new.

> with a real desire to change, you can add the future intention

Putting the statements into the past tense suggests that there is a *possibility* things can change now and in the future. To create a real change in behaviour, you have to work on designing the future. For that to happen, there has to be a real desire to bring it about. With a real desire to change, you can add the future intention. For example, a person with a real desire to build a relationship with his manager might say, 'In the past, my manager and I have had our differences, but I am going to make a real effort to listen and understand his point of view.'

Similarly, the person having difficulty with arithmetic, but with a real desire to keep the household accounts in order, might say, 'In the past, I have had some challenges with arithmetic, but I am going to take some lessons and practise adding up so that I can keep on top of my finances.'

We encourage you to listen closely to the words people say and to your own internal dialogue, and to challenge it where appropriate using the metamodel questions.

Using metaphors to create change

Further insight into the ways people think can be gained by observing what metaphors they use. Metaphors are also very effective tools when pacing and leading other people.

Some people have a way of using metaphors that gives away their map of reality. Some such patterns have become part of the everyday language we all use. Here are some common examples:

- 'It's like watching paint dry.'
- 'She was like a bull in a china shop.'
- 'This is the Rolls-Royce edition.'
- 'It's like walking through treacle.'
- 'We need to ride the storm.'

Metaphors like these are a manifestation of a map of reality. Identifying with a person's metaphor can create instant rapport. You can pace and lead someone effectively and elegantly by picking up on their metaphors without even knowing the true content of their meaning. Here is an example from a conversation between David and Ben.

brilliant example

Ben:	It's like the car is running, the wheels are going round, but we're not going anywhere.
David:	Really! That must mean the engine's working very hard.
Ben:	You're right, it is.
David:	Then that must be putting a lot of strain on the engine.
Ben:	You are absolutely right – it's like there is so much detail and I can't join up the dots.
David:	Which dots?
Ben:	The dots of my aspiration.
David:	What do the dots look like?
Ben:	I don't know – actually there aren't any.

In this conversation, David first joined Ben in his metaphor. He then led him from a state of frustration to a realisation that his stress was of his own making. Ben didn't know where his stress was coming from. By developing the metaphor, he became aware that the cause of his stress was an aspiration without a plan.

Persuading with elegance

It is easy to let words pass as the urgency to 'have your say' takes over. Every word can have an impact. Are your words having the impact you want?

> if you ... practise them, you will be able to influence and persuade elegantly

The aspects of language covered in this chapter give you options as to how you communicate. If you remember and practise them, you will be able to influence and persuade elegantly.

Because language has such an immediate impact, you will find that your words will increase your personal power in such areas as:

- getting your ideas across
- coaching others
- working with groups
- presenting in public
- teaching
- negotiating
- parenting
- working through personal problems.

Above all, it will give you more confidence and positive energy in all areas of your life.

brilliant tip

The secret of effective questioning is to choose the one question that is absolutely appropriate to create a shift in someone's thinking. If we constantly ask questions just because we can, we will very soon become 'Billy no mates'.

brilliant recap

In this chaper you have learned that:

- your language is a surface-level communication of a deeper real-world experience and it contains generalisations, deletions and distortions of your original experience
- your language contains various patterns of communication,

some of which are beliefs about the world; some beliefs act as limitations and barriers to developing potential

- learning the metamodel can help to overcome limiting beliefs
- the metamodel questions can be used with equal effectiveness with your own internal dialogue
- a person's language contains many metaphors which can be utilised to influence them.

CHAPTER 8

The impact of emotion on time

n Chapter 2 we described the difference between in-time and thru-time metaprogrammes and the implications of both. Let's recap briefly. *In-time* refers to being fully in the moment. *Thru-time* refers to being somewhat dissociated from the moment as the immediate past and future are afforded a higher value and take up a good proportion of the person's thinking. Our relationship with time plays such a large part in our lives that we feel this particular topic merits a chapter of its own.

Contrary to popular belief, time is an emotional issue, not a practical one. Just think back to a time when you realised you ought to be getting on with something important, but procrastinated. How did you feel at the time? I expect you were mentally disconnected from the task, but emotionally connected with the bad feeling about procrastinating! Time management courses consist of the application of various practical systems for structuring your day, week, month and year, by prioritising, but no amount of colour coding, listmaking or prioritising is going to solve an emotionally-based issue. In our experience, most people who live mainly in-time rarely benefit from conventional time management training and people who live mainly thru-time rarely need it as they have a natural ability to plan and schedule.

> time is an emotional issue, not a practical one

brilliant example

Tina had a strong tendency to be thru-time. The value she put on planning and getting things done was so great that it outweighed any need she had for forming professional relationships. People where she worked felt undervalued by her and developed the habit of putting her requirements to the bottom of their list of things to do. This caused time delays for Tina's projects and she became frustrated at her inability to meet deadlines. The more Tina became frustrated, the more she blamed her colleagues for their ineptness and the worse the problem became.

Through coaching, Tina balanced her approach to time. She learned to create more in-time moments, focusing on her professional relationships and, before long, people were prioritising her work requests more positively.

Let's take a closer look at in-time and thru-time patterns.

In-time, thru-time and your timeline

Time is a metaphor. Humans invented it to help coordinate activities, but, even so, we tend to think of our own lives as a linear sequence of growth and maturity, and most planning systems progress from left to right as a sequence of hours, days, weeks, months and years.

The easiest way to think about your relationship with time is as an invisible line going from past, through the present and on into the future. If you were to think about this line tracing a path from past to future in relation to your body, it may look something like one of the two common time configurations shown opposite.

Of course, these are not the only two configurations and, in our work, we have come across some extraordinary timelines that work for people in different ways. For the moment, though, let's consider the implications of these two variations.

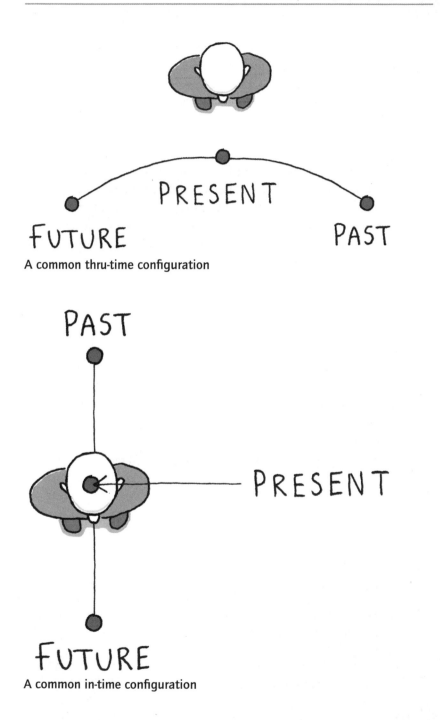

A common thru-time configuration

A common in-time configuration

It stands to reason that the thru-time configuration gives a person a clear view of the past and the future. He or she can actually visualise past and future events as if images of the memories were stored on the line itself. The fact that the line is to the front of the body explains the often dissociated perspective that an extreme thru-time pattern can generate.

Conversely, the in-time configuration puts the past behind the person, in a place where it cannot easily be seen, and the future straight ahead, where only the immediate moment is visible – that is, now. Is it any wonder, therefore, that people with this configuration are absorbed in the present and cannot foresee what is going to happen next?

🎬 brilliant example

Sobia had a zest for life that was admired by all her friends. She loved starting projects, but her in-time approach to life wreaked havoc as she moved from one project to another, openly displaying her excitement and underestimating the time that each one would take. Consequently, she frequently let people down as she was unable to keep to the strenuous time schedule she set for herself. Because she was fun to be around, her friends simply put it down to scattiness and developed the habit of making allowances for her.

Here is a series of exercises that you can do to help balance your timeline.

Establishing your current position

First, decide where your issues with time lie and what they are related to by doing the following:

1 Write a list of:
    a   the things you spend your time doing

b   what you should be doing but never get around to

c   what you would like to do but don't, for whatever
     reason.

2   Mark each activity according to its enjoyment factor, on a
     scale where 0 = least enjoyable and 10 = most enjoyable.

3   Take a look at each activity that scored above 5 on your
     enjoyment scale and ask yourself whether you do it to avoid
     doing something else or because it is a useful part of your
     daily productivity. That includes activities for relaxation
     and fitness, as they are very important to your health.

4   Now look at the activities that scored below 5. What's
     stopping you from enjoying them? Is it a relationship
     problem, a skill set problem or a metaprogramme conflict,
     as highlighted in Chapter 2?

5   Select two or three activities that you would like to change
     in some way and decide on a course of action. For example,
     if you need more confidence, you could set yourself an
     anchor or collapse an old anchor. You could use the new
     behaviour generator exercise in Chapter 13 to rebuild a
     relationship once you have spent some time working out
     what caused the relationship to falter in the first place.

If you have an extreme in-time or thru-time metaprogramme,
here are some ways you can balance them.

Balancing a thru-time line

Because time is a metaphor, and all timelines are imaginary,
they can be easily changed using some simple techniques. When
a thru-time line is overly dominant, as in the first brilliant
example, it can cause unnecessary stress. Balancing it involves
a simple breathing technique that allows you to remain present
in the moment instead of mentally performing your next task or
reviewing the one you did yesterday.

1   Take a deep breath and place the forefinger and thumb of
    either hand over your heart area.

2   Look down and to the right while telling yourself, 'This
    moment is very important to achieving my desired outcome
    [name it here]'. Exhale as you do this.

3   Feel your chest sinking as you exhale, then slowly look up
    and continue with your activity, feeling more connected
    with the people around you.

Balancing an in-time line

A common habit related to an in-time line is the tendency to
vastly underestimate how long things really take and spend
longer than necessary doing them.

It is possible to 'rebuild' a timeline to give you a more accurate
perspective of how long things will take, but, in order for it to
work, you need to really want to make this change.

1   Find a quiet place and imagine physically picking up your
    timeline and swinging it around in front of you, then
    stepping back so that you can see it clearly stretching from
    left to right. To make this clearer, give the line some kind of
    colour or form – perhaps making it wider, shiny, metallic or
    furry – whatever works for you.

2   Now take yourself back into the past and select a pleasant
    memory from when you were about five years old. Make
    the picture clear, bright and colourful, then place it to the
    far left of your line. Repeat this for when you were 10, then
    15 and so on, right up to the present day.

3   Now think about your plans for the future. Create a
    pleasurable image of what you will be doing tomorrow
    – make it big, bright and colourful, then place it on
    the timeline in the appropriate place. Do the same for

something you will be doing next week, next month, in six months' time and as far as you want to go.

4   Review all the images for a while so that, when you want to access them, they pop up into your mind's eye at the places where you put them. The more you practise, the easier it will become.

5   When you want to plan something, create a pleasant mental image of the activity and place it on your new timeline in an appropriate place. Review it daily.

Creating a mental calendar

An in-time line can often be the cause of a bad memory for future events, such as birthdays and meetings. People who are good at carrying dates like these in their heads often use a visual system to help them. Here's one way you can develop this ability:

1   Create a visual image to represent the hours in the day. This can be a calendar page divided into hours or a computer-generated image of your electronic calendar. If you prefer, create it in linear form if that works for you. Make the image bright, clear and colourful.

2   Mentally place all the activities you are going to be involved in tomorrow on the page. You can either write them clearly or use bright pictures to represent each activity.

3   Do the same for next week, only this time you can put in a little less detail. If there are days you haven't yet planned for, then see them as blank spaces – make sure they are included and that the spaces represent the length of time available.

4   Now have a go at creating next month. With a little practice you will learn to sense the amount of time various activities will take and be able to plan your time more effectively.

If you have not yet developed a strong visual imagination, you can develop it through frequent practice.

The calendar creation exercise is not something we made up but what many people, who know nothing about NLP, do naturally. We modelled it from them. Creating a mental calendar is as natural a skill as any other mental function, and anyone can learn to do it.

brilliant tip

Some people create their mental calendars using the imagery of a personal computer. The proliferation of computers and Windows software has influenced the imaginations of people everywhere. The function of clicking on a button to expand an image can be used to bring up mental images by clicking an imaginary button and then they can be collapsed in the same way. This is not so peculiar when you think that Windows software was created by a human mind to reflect how a human mind works with visual images.

We encourage you to explore your mind's ability to create formats for representing time with creative enthusiasm.

brilliant recap

In this chapter you have learned that:

- there are two main ways of experiencing time, *in-time* (being in the moment) and *through-time* (being very aware of the passing of time); people tend to have their own unique mix of both, some mainly preferring one over the other
- a person's timeline configuration may be the cause of poor time management

- the concept of time creates an emotional connection with the world around you; whether you will be early or late to an event will have a direct impact on your emotional state

- we tend to perceive time as travelling from past to future in a left to right direction (look at any chart showing time on the axis)

- time is a metaphor and, as such, each person creates their unique metaphor of time

- a person's unique experience of time is called their timeline

- because time is a metaphor, you can change your timeline.

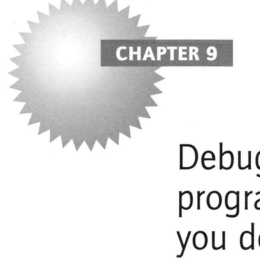

CHAPTER 9

Debug the programmes you don't want

You have now covered all the main components that are involved in the way you communicate with yourself and others. The diagram on the next page shows how NLP puts it all together.

By generalising, deleting and distorting information, you create your own unique personal map of reality that you represent in your mind with imagery and sounds (smell and taste may also feature).

The result of this 'internal representation of reality' is a range of feelings. You have probably said to yourself on certain occasions, 'I'm not in the right state of mind for this job right now'. That state of mind is actually a mind–body state, as the feelings responsible for it are not just in the head, but throughout your body. The state is caused by your personal map of reality, so, if you tell yourself that so-and-so is making you stressed, a state will be created and you will begin to feel tense, which will show in your behaviour. Likewise, if you feel intimidated by someone, the state created will result in behaviour that affects your ability to respond effectively.

You will see from the diagram that your state also affects your physiology. So, if you feel threatened and in a state of fear, you will try to make your body smaller to avoid the situation. This is a natural reaction to any threat, whether it is a physical one or a direct challenge to your authority by a more senior person. Of course, some people might react the opposite way, facing the

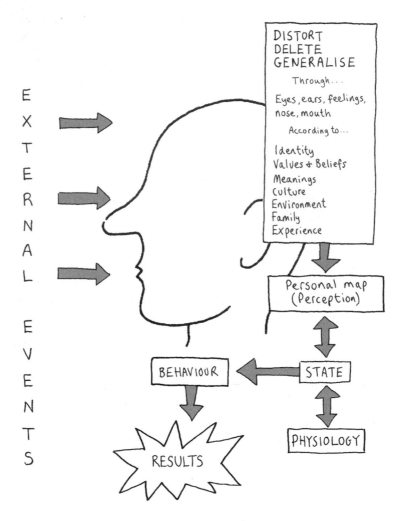

challenge head-on. How you react to this or any type of situation depends on how you are creating your personal map of reality.

You will also notice in the diagram that your physiology also affects your state. That is why doctors often recommend physical exercise, such as running, for patients exhibiting signs of depression. Getting energy moving around the body has a positive effect on your mental state. You can use this technique, too, to get out of a negative state and give yourself a lift. You can also use deep breathing to calm yourself down. NLP utilises all the ways in which the mind and body affect each other.

This mind–body interaction is exactly the same in whatever state you create for yourself – it begins with your personal map. So, checking all the different aspects of your personal map, and making changes to create more positive and useful states, such as confidence, calm, focus, excitement, enthusiasm, persistence and so on, is at the core of NLP. That is how your programmes are formed and how you change them.

You have programmes for everything you do – motivating yourself, procrastinating, negotiating, getting tired, buying things. You also have programmes for all the things you would rather *not* do but continue with because you have formed a strong habit of doing them. All the programmes consist of sequences of thoughts and behaviour that are triggered by certain stimuli. In NLP, each sequence is called a 'strategy' for achieving an outcome. If you have ever tried to break a habit and failed, then it is more than likely that you were unaware of either the trigger or the unconscious parts of the strategy. Once you know about all the components of a strategy, you can do any number of things, including:

> once you know about all the components of a strategy, you can do any number of things

- changing it for something more useful
- copying an effective strategy from someone else
- designing a new one from scratch.

brilliant example

Dennis was very careful with his money. When he made a decision to buy something, he would follow a set strategy. It went something like this:

- visualise myself using it (internal visual)
- ask, 'Do I really need it?' (internal dialogue)
- if the answer is 'Yes', research the model/type/make/price (internal visual)
- ask, 'Who shall I ask for an opinion?' (internal dialogue based on external reference metaprogramme)
- 'Ask Jack and Bob' (external auditory)
- say, 'Yes, that feels right' (kinaesthetic)
- ask, 'Where shall I buy it from?' (internal dialogue)
- consider Internet/shop/mail order (internal visual)
- say, 'Yes, that feels right' (kinaesthetic)
- buy!

Compare this with Beverley's strategy:

- say, 'That would look great on me' (external visual)
- try it on (external kinaesthetic)
- say, 'Looks good, feels good' (external visual and external kinaesthetic)
- buy!

Some people who are good at spelling use a strategy consisting of visual pictures of the letters placed in the correct order, usually brightly coloured. A common reason for some people not being good spellers is that they don't use such a good strategy. Poor spellers often try to spell by pronouncing words using their internal dialogue. Anyone can be a good speller – you just have to learn an effective strategy using visuals of words and not just what they sound like.

The TOTE model

Whether it's spelling, getting rich, finding a partner, buying something, learning a skill, getting a better job or being fitter and healthier, NLP gives you the models and techniques to be aware of what could be limiting you and the tools to change the situation.

One of the models for improving your success in all these areas and more is the TOTE model, which stands for:

- Test
- Operate
- Test
- Exit.

This is the minimum number of steps involved in any process of decision making that begins with some kind of trigger causing you to make a decision. You will see from the model on the next page that there is a central point where people often get stuck in a loop.

You may have heard people quoting the following: 'If you always do what you have always done you will always get what you have always got', 'Doing the same thing and expecting different results is a sign of madness' or 'If you want to change your results do something different'. Well, these quotes all relate to the TOTE model, which originates from G. A. Gallanter, E. Pribram and K. H. Miller who described it in their 1960 book *Plans and the Structure of Behaviour* (Holt, Reinhart and Winston). The model fits very well with the core principles of NLP and you can use it to become more aware of your own decision process.

Ineffective strategies prevent people from achieving so many things. How well do you manage your finances? What about the presentations you have given? How well do you communicate with people at work? Are you a good cook? What about the way you make decisions? Can you maintain positive and fruitful relationships?

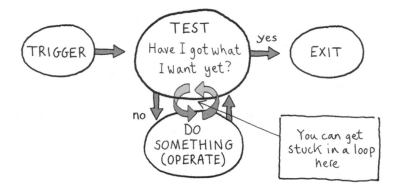

Let's take a typical ineffective behaviour as an example to see how the TOTE model works. How about intimidation? This usually means being in a situation where another person is acting in a way that causes you to feel inadequate and at loss for an effective response. So you decide that you are not going to be intimidated any more and think through what you are going to say the next time you meet the intimidating person. Next time comes and you blurt out what you have rehearsed (your Operation), but the other person comes back with an even stronger response and you crawl back into your shell. You might repeat this strategy any number of times, each time thinking of what else you can say: you are stuck in the TOTE loop.

To Exit the loop, you need to do something different. You need to develop a much stronger feeling of self-confidence, such that, no matter what anyone says, you will remain unaffected by it. You may also need a more effective system of language that doesn't depend on remembering to say one rehearsed thing. The NLP metamodel described in Chapter 7 is ideal for this purpose.

There is another saying that you may also have heard: 'You don't know what you don't know'. It refers to the fact that many people struggle with everyday situations in life and work, stuck in TOTE loops because they don't know that there are skills that can help them to make an Exit. Many people struggle to give a formal presentation not knowing that a little NLP could make the experience highly rewarding and positive. Managers struggle to motivate their teams because they don't know that there are skills they can learn to do this, and they can enjoy it. If you believe that good leaders are born and not made, your personal map will prevent you from exploring the possibility that effective leadership can be learned and enjoyed.

Whatever aspect of your life you want to improve, you can bet there is a strategy you are currently using that is holding you back, either creating inertia or producing undesirable results. The key is to know the beginning and end of each strategy so that you can change it.

Eliciting a strategy

When you elicit a strategy, you will discover values, beliefs and metaprogrammes, plus a sequence of thoughts, behaviour and physiological aspects, such as muscle tightness, posture, breathing rate, and so on.

Eliciting a strategy

Choose something you do that you would rather not do or something you would like to improve on - motivating yourself, stopping procrastinating, improving your decision making or giving up smoking, for example.

Find the trigger

- How do you know when to do this?

▶

- What lets you know you are ready to do this?
- What do you do as you are preparing to … ?
- What steps do you go through?
- What happens next?
- Then what happens?
- How do you know when you have succeeded?
- How do you test whether or not you have succeeded?
- What lets you know that you have not yet succeeded?

Check the strategy

When you have elicited the complete strategy, repeat it back to check if anything is missing. If you want to change it, the place to do this is at the trigger point. The object is not to remove the original strategy but, rather, create an alternative choice, as the strategy may be useful in other contexts.

brilliant example

Norman wanted to stop smoking. He could manage without a cigarette most of the time, but found the urge irresistible when he had something to celebrate. At such times, his strategy included a visual of his hero on top of a mountain smoking a cigarette. This resulted in a strong belief that 'all successful people smoke', hence his need to smoke when he felt successful.

Once Norman realised that was his trigger, he changed his belief to 'no matter how successful you are, smart people don't smoke'. He was then able to modify his strategy at the trigger point, removing the cigarette from the visual of his hero. As a consequence, he lost the urge to smoke.

Creating a new strategy

1 Think of a strategy that you would like to have. For example:

- getting out of bed with a spring in your step
- losing weight
- keeping fit
- arriving home after work feeling energetic
- getting to sleep
- doing your accounts
- paying the bills
- helping the children with their homework
- improving your sports performance.

2 Create strong *values* and rock-solid *beliefs* – stated in the positive – about the desire to have the strategy. For example, 'When I have this strategy, I will be able to do/have ...' or 'I really want this strategy because ...' and 'I can be/do ... whenever I choose to be/do ...'.

3 Decide on the trigger for your strategy. For example, if you want to lose weight, it could be whenever the thought of food crosses your mind, it is time to prepare a meal or sit at the table.

4 Create a powerful series of images of you succeeding with the strategy. Break it down step by step, making each image big, bright and colourful. Keep the images dissociated and use strong, empowering internal dialogue.

5 Mentally practise your new strategy in slow motion as many times as it takes to programme your thinking.

6 Test the strategy by imagining a time in the future when you will want to use it. Run through it in your mind.

brilliant tip

When you first work with strategies, there is a tendency to work with *big* chunks. The key to changing a strategy, though, can lie in a quick internal visual or in exaggerating or removing internal dialogue. Keeping to *small* chunks will allow you to access the essential finer details. Also, pay attention to the trigger point for a strategy – accessing the trigger point is vital to changing any strategy.

brilliant recap

In this chapter you have learned that:

- sequences of thinking and behaviour, which tend to be repeated, can be considered as 'strategies'
- all sequences have a trigger point which is a response to an inner or outer stimulus
- everything you do, including making decisions; shopping; choosing a partner; learning a new skill; having feelings of guilt, anxiety, fear or excitement, etc, begins with a triggered response and is repeated with precision by a strategy
- a strategy contains the following elements: a sequence of vak cognitive distinctions, one or more values and associated beliefs, metaprogrammes and physiology
- the TOTE model is used to understand how strategies can loop and have an exit point once a condition is met
- strategies can be elicited and changed
- brand new strategies can be created.

CHAPTER 10

Fantastic outcomes

n Chapter 5 we introduced the five levels of alignment. We suggested that, for you to live a happy and fulfilled life, all the levels have to be aligned. What actually happens is that, no matter how well aligned you think you are, life has ways of enticing you to become misaligned. The decisions you make every day will either pull you closer to being aligned or push you further away from this ideal. Sometimes, you can have all your levels lined up but still feel a tug. This can happen if your outcome is not clearly defined.

> no matter how well aligned you think you are, life has ways of enticing you to become misaligned

NLP has an approach to setting goals called 'well-formed outcomes'. For example, if you are about to make an important telephone call or apply for a new job or promotion, have you thought through the possible outcomes? What is your ideal outcome for attending the sales meeting next week? What is your intended outcome for spending time with your children? What is the outcome you would like when you have that night out with your friends? What outcome are you aiming for with your new business idea, joining the squash club or taking up t'ai chi or yoga?

Once you have established a clear outcome, you can decide what role you will play, establish your values and beliefs concerning the situation, develop your capabilities, adjust your behaviour and have a positive impact on your surroundings.

Do I need a purpose or an outcome?

Think of 'purpose' as being at a higher level than 'identity' – more about the essence of who you are than a description of your role.

brilliant example

Colin described his role as 'a life coach working with people to facilitate positive personal change'. He described his purpose as being 'to help people realise their true potential'. As he goes about his work as a life coach, Colin keeps this purpose at the forefront of his mind. The outcome he wants for each session, however, will depend on the individual needs of his client.

A strong sense of purpose provides you with the energy to move forward with certainty and confidence. Outcomes focus on being clear about your desired results in specific situations.

> outcomes differ from goals ... by setting outcomes, there is so much more you can achieve

Outcomes differ from goals in that a goal usually takes the form of a short statement about what you want to achieve. An outcome considers other consequences of the effort applied to achieve the goal. When you merely state a goal, then that is what you measure. By setting outcomes, there is so much more you can achieve.

brilliant example

Tim set a goal to increase new account sales by 15 per cent by the end of the quarter. His outcomes, as a result of having achieved the increase, were 'for his team to feel good about their contribution, the new clients to be happy with the service, potential for further added-value sales and the team to have learned more about selling and influencing.'

Making sure that your outcomes are well formed

The acronym PRIEST provides a framework for determining the strength and validity of any outcome to ensure that it is well formed.

P is for positively stated

A feature of the human mind is its inability to process a negative. Consider the instruction, 'Whatever you do, do *not* think about a pink elephant.' Oh! Too late, you thought about one, didn't you? We know you did because you *have* to think of the thing you are not supposed to think about!

Beware your capacity to 'get what you focus on'. If your main focus is on what you *don't* want, you may end up getting it. To avoid this, make sure that your outcomes are clearly stated in the positive. In other words, say what you *do* want, not what you *don't* want (a pink elephant).

> beware your capacity to 'get what you focus on'

R is for resources

This includes internal as well as external resources. Do you have the courage, confidence, staying power, commitment, determination and other internal resources you may need to succeed?

If not, there are NLP techniques you can use to acquire them. What external resources will you need – finance, people, knowledge?

I is for initiated and maintained by self

Is the achievement of the outcome totally in your control or does it depend on something outside it?

You may want to adjust your outcome if you are not fully in control. Even if you have other people to help you, make sure that you keep hold of the responsibility for your choices – whether things go according to plan or not.

E is for ecology

Have you considered the consequences of achieving your outcome? What are the likely impacts on other people and other aspects of your life? Are they acceptable to you?

This is known as an 'ecology check'.

S is for sensory evidence

What sensory evidence will tell you that you have successfully achieved your outcomes? What will you hear? What will you see and how will you feel?

Take some time to imagine how things will be in the future, having achieved what you set out to achieve. How will you know that you have been successful?

T is for time

What timescale are you working to? How long will it take you to achieve all the outcomes attached to your goal?

If you write out your goals, it is very easy to miss something. The following exercise uses space and visualisation to help you set a realistic timescale and check how well formed your outcomes really are.

Visualise your success

Find a quiet space where you can visualise your journey of achievement.

Mark a space on the floor to represent 'now'. From this space, walk to a point on the floor a particular distance away to represent the time you think it will take you to achieve your outcomes. Stand on that point and look back at 'now'. Spend some time feeling what it's like to have achieved all of your outcomes.

Next, walk a little further into the future and turn around. Look back at 'now' again and visualise what you did to achieve your outcomes. Make sure that your internal language is in the past tense. Once your mind has grasped the idea that you have *already* succeeded, visualising what you *did* as opposed to what you *have to do* is a much more creative, insightful and far less stressful process. It's very powerful and great fun, too.

brilliant example

Linda likes to look after people and entertain. Her outcome for a night out was to make sure that Joy enjoyed her birthday after a period of illness (positively stated).

Linda booked Joy's favourite restaurant, made sure all the guests were happy to contribute to the event, took responsibility (initiated by self) for making sure that the guests knew the location, where to park and gave them an arrival time and a dress code (internal and external resources). She checked that Joy's health was up to such a night (ecology). Linda created an image in her mind of the guests leaving the restaurant smiling and laughing and Joy sitting happily at the table having had a wonderful evening (sensory-based evidence).

The schedule of things to do before the event helped it run smoothly and allowed Linda to enjoy the evening as much as Joy (timing). A hostess with real purpose and drive!

Consider what the consequences of *not* having well-formed outcomes to achieve her goal would have been. She might have left preparations to the last minute, found Joy's favourite restaurant to be fully booked, spent the hours before the event taking phone calls from guests needing directions, ▶

felt bad and had to apologise to Joy for not having booked her favourite restaurant and arrived in a flustered state, unable to give Joy and the guests her attention.

How well everyday experiences like this go makes a big difference to your energy and results. Taking the PRIEST approach helps with the present and opens up future possibilities. Linda's reputation for organising events calmly and effectively is a skill that she can apply to other areas of her life, including her work and family. When you work with outcomes in this way, you generate positive energy that will attract positive people to you.

brilliant example

Despite an underprivileged upbringing, Tom has an unstoppable sense of purpose. Combining his skills as an expressive dancer with his ability to teach dance as a way of helping youngsters to be confident and believe in themselves, he embarked on a mission.

When we met Tom, he had a very clear outcome in mind: he wanted to establish a dancing competition that enabled teams from schools around London to choreograph and perform their own dance creations. They would then enter a series of qualifying events and the teams chosen for the final would have the opportunity to dance on stage at Olympia.

Tom took on the role of organiser and his values concerning the young people and creative expression held him in good stead. He worked on his self-belief and quickly acquired the internal resources of confidence and determination he needed to turn the idea into a series of actions. From there on, he knew where to find the external resources he needed and took control of the entire project. Tom knew exactly what he would hear, see and feel when the event was successful.

Six months later, hundreds of highly expressive youngsters took to the stage at the first Olympiada ever in the UK. It was a great success.

Putting everything together to create a brilliant future

If you have followed all the steps in this book, you now have everything you need to create a brilliant future for yourself.

The next exercise gives you a structure for choosing which techniques are appropriate to make the desired changes. It can be used in conjunction with the PRIEST exercise or on its own as a way of becoming aligned with a personal change you want to make. It is used here along with the PRIEST exercise. As you proceed, there are suggested techniques you may wish to use, some of which you have covered in previous sections of the book, while others are in Chapter 13.

Creating a brilliant future

1 Prepare a set of cards or sheets of paper marked as follows:

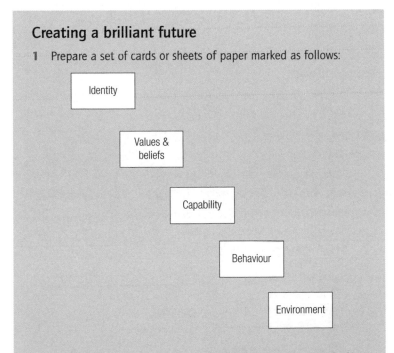

2 Sit in a quiet place, relax and look up. Create an image of what life will be like at some point in the future. Choose a period

when you have achieved one or more of the outcomes that are important to you now.

3   Mark two spots on the floor – one to represent today and one for a time in the future when you will have achieved a specific outcome. The distance (time) between the two spots should be what feels right. Stand on the future spot and imagine what it is like. Imagine you have a remote control like the one you use for your television. Use it to intensify the qualities of your internal imagery and sound. Turn up the brightness, increase the colour, improve the contrast, make it bigger and bring it closer. Turn up the volume and listen to the sounds. Have the sound tuned so that there is no interference. Step into the picture and notice the feelings of satisfaction and achievement. Enjoy the moment and anchor this state.

Technique used

● Anchoring.

4   Lay the cards you made above, in the same order, at equal intervals between where you are standing now ('future') and the spot representing 'today'.

5   Stand at a point just beyond the 'future' spot and look back at 'today'. Fire the anchor you set earlier. How does it feel, having achieved your outcome(s)? From this position, what have you got to say to the you of 'today'? Have you any tips or advice?

6   Move to the 'Identity' card. Ask yourself how you have changed, now that you have achieved your outcome(s). What is different about you? What role are you now playing that you were not playing before?

FUTURE

IDENTITY

VALUES & BELIEFS

CAPABILITY

BEHAVIOUR

ENVIRONMENT

TODAY

7 Move to the 'Values & beliefs' card. What values have you changed, if any, and how have your beliefs changed in order to achieve this success?

Techniques used

● Values elicitation

● Belief change

● Reframing

● This not that

● Metamodel.

8 Move to the 'Capability' spot. How have your capabilities changed? What did you learn along the way?

Technique used

● Artfully vague language.

9 Move to the 'Behaviour' card. What did you do along the way? What are you doing differently now?

Techniques used

● New behaviour generator (in Chapter 13)

● Collapsing anchors

● Anchoring

● PRIEST

● Strategies.

10 Move on to the 'Environment' card. What impact has achieving your outcome(s) had on those around you? Is your environment still the same or has it changed at all? If so, how?

Technique used

● Perceptual positions (in Chapter 13).

11 Revisit the cards in any order you wish if you feel that there is still work to do. You will know when you have true alignment as, then, all the tugs will have disappeared and you will have a burning desire to make your first move.

Spacing the cards out on the floor helps you to 'programme in' the changes you want to make and gives you a better concept of space and time than if you just did the exercise mentally. If you have completed the exercise correctly, there is no need to write anything down – you will then have integrated it firmly and clearly.

brilliant tip

Begin thinking about future goals as if you have already achieved them. Ask yourself what the outcomes were. Try this with, for example, making a telephone call, going to a meeting, having a touchy conversation with your partner, buying a new house or car. Assume that the event has passed and you were successful. What are the outcomes? What have you achieved? Make the answers to these questions your focus as you work towards achieving them for real.

brilliant recap

In this chapter you have learned that:

- creating well-formed outcomes for the things you want to achieve will help you to achieve more

- outcomes have a wider impact than goals as they include consequences and ecology

- you can be more effective in all that you do by defining outcomes

- it is easy to work out how to achieve an outcome when you trick yourself into believing it is already accomplished – look back to see how you did it

- you can use the acronym PRIEST to define a well-formed outcome.

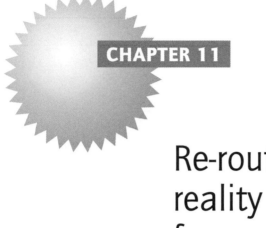

CHAPTER 11

Re-route your
reality map
for possibility

Neuroscientists refer to the mind as the most powerful computer on Earth. It has over 10 billion neurons and is capable of making more connections than all the telephone systems in the entire world, yet your mind, like all minds, has its limitations.

It *must* have limitations because, just as a telephone system would overload if everyone placed a call at the same time, you would eventually blow a fuse or have a mental breakdown if you attempted to take in everything that is going on in your world. Just try listening to two people talking at the same time and you will realise how easily such an overload could happen. We have already explained how we deal with this – through a process of generalising, distorting and deleting – in order to make our information processing more compact and manageable. As we do this we go through three fundamental steps:

1 taking in information

 through the senses

2 assimilating and processing the information

 attaching meanings, judgements and opinions

3 communicating the results to other people and acting in accordance with our meanings, judgements and opinions

 what we say and how we come across to others.

By now you know that your beliefs and values influence this process. What you believe to be right, proper, sensible, appropriate and allowable occurs as a necessary part of filtering information and putting it into a structure to help you make day-to-day decisions. You create a set of decision-making rules and, for many people, the more experience they have, the bigger their list of rules. By the time some people have reached 40 years of age, their lists of rules allow little possibility for new experiences. This is like locking yourself up in jail in order to limit your freedom, which is the cause of many a teenager's angst. While the body is not physically restricted, the mind is shackled as a result of all the self-imposed rules collected over time, and the body suffers as a result.

---

brilliant example

Nina wouldn't allow herself to do any of the things that she really wanted to, such as take a flight in an aeroplane and visit another country. Even though she talked endlessly about wanting to do so, she would always add at the end of her sentence, 'I'm too nervous to fly, though, and other countries are not very safe these days.'

> rules should allow you to make smart choices, not limit your potential

Rules should allow you to make smart choices, not limit your potential and restrict your freedom.

What you accept from society as a result of your daily experiences, together with media influences, will build on this rule structure. Add to this your views on life, ageing, health, diet, education, travel, employment, family, individuality, youth culture, politics, religion and technology and you can see how the structure gets more complex, with even more rules. The tendency then is to avoid overload by further generalisation, deletion and distortion.

We are brought up and educated to have a view on things, to be a person with opinions because opinions shape the world, but opinions can also limit our progress, learning and ability to adapt and change.

brilliant example

Lesley runs a family hotel business that is struggling to attract new guests. Her bank manager tried to help her by offering ideas on how to improve the customer experience. His intentions were positive, but Lesley was having none of it. She accused her banker of having no experience relevant to customer service and so he was not in a position to help. Lesley felt threatened by him and became defensive, quoting all the things she believed had to happen in order for the hotel to work – rules that she had created about what could and couldn't happen in the hotel and what was and wasn't possible. The consequence of her 'working to rule' had a negative impact on customer service, but she wasn't going to change.

Lesley, who had rarely travelled outside her home town of Blackpool, had allowed her rules to take over. She had missed an ideal opportunity to draw on the 10 years' experience the bank manager had of travelling the world, staying in a variety of quality hotels and being on the receiving end of varying levels of customer service.

Your reality map

All your rules combine to create a map, like a route map, you use every day to make decisions that shape your future and determine your direction in life. The question to ask is, 'How rich is your route map?' When you look at your map can you see the limitations you have set for yourself in the following three key relationship areas?

- The relationships you allow and deny yourself with other people.
- The relationships you allow and deny yourself with your work.
- The relationship you allow and deny with yourself.

Think about these three sets of relationships for a while, one at a time. Reflect on the rules you have created that perhaps allow only a certain type of relationship to form and deny other possible forms of relationship.

Now let's take a few life categories and consider the rules you have created within each of them that form either a rich or poor route map. While going through the list that follows, remember you need rules in order to exist from day to day, but there are rules that limit your potential and rules that keep you open to the world of possibility. There is a big difference between the two examples of rules that follow. Imagine what each person might allow and deny themselves as a result of their rule.

- Person a: 'Professional qualifications are required to get on in the world today.'
- Person b: 'Everyone and every experience teaches me new things every day.'

you can have any rules you want

Imagine having *both* rules. Why not? You can have any rules you want. You don't have to stick with the ones you have now.

Go through the following lists, taking one question at a time and considering each in terms of a rule. The objective is to challenge your existing rules and know that you can have any rules you want.

Education

- Do you believe that there is a limit to what you can learn?

- Do you believe that education is more about knowledge or experience?
- At what age do you consider education to be completed?
- What does education have to do with passing exams?
- How many happy and successful people do you know who have not followed your rules about education?
- What rules about education would give you the best opportunity to learn new things?
- What do you include in the term 'education'?

Health and fitness

- Do you count your age in numbers, one extra for each birthday?
- When you reach each birthday, do you celebrate getting older or wiser or something else?
- Do you have a view as to how long you are likely to live? If so, where has that view come from?
- What do you believe about your ability to have a healthy lifestyle?
- Is it important to keep fit?
- Which is more important, your work or your health?
- Do you have a view on how your health and lifestyle will determine how long you live?
- What are your views on diet? Where did they come from?
- Do you think that your attitude has an influence on your health?

Social norms

- Are you comfortable going against the grain?
- Do you dress more to please yourself or to fit in with what others are wearing?

- What do you think of people who refuse to follow the herd?
- What do you like about the culture of your country?
- What do you dislike about the culture of your country?
- Do you enjoy visiting different cultures?
- What did you think of when answering the previous question?
- What's your view on youth culture?
- How did you form your view of youth culture?
- What do you think about people who jump queues and break rules?
- What social norms can you think of that you conform to without question?

Other people

- Do you tend to trust people when you first meet them or do they have to earn your trust?
- How did you arrive at the rule above?
- Do you think that people should look out for one another or be self-sufficient?
- What is behind your answer to the above question?
- Do you think that people are generally becoming more generous or greedier, a mix of the two or something else?
- What did you think of in order to answer the question above?

Job or career

- Is it important to enjoy your job?
- Do you think it's more important that people get on with each other at work or compete for the best jobs?
- What's most important, having a job or having a career?

- Is there any stage in life where a career change isn't sensible?
- Rank the following in terms of requirements to be successful in any job:
  - qualifications
  - experience
  - right attitude
  - good communication and team-working ability.
- What thought process did you go through to answer the above question?
- What's more important:
  - mathematical ability
  - an appreciation of art and being artistic?

How did it go? Did some questions cause you to think more deeply than others? Which ones were the easiest to answer? The easiest ones will be those for which you already have a rule. Where you had to think more, you probably have no hard rule or your answer would depend on other circumstances not offered in the question.

---

brilliant example

Tom, a highly educated chemical engineer, was being mentored by his CEO who saw potential for a top management role. Unfortunately, he was becoming increasingly unpopular amongst the senior team as a result of him pushing his ideas onto them. They responded by cutting him out of the communication on important projects. This caused Tom a high degree of frustration. During a coaching session he realised that he was operating out of a rule that 'people should do what's obviously the right thing and not get drawn into politics'. The flaw here is clearly that his rule is not helping, and when frustration sets in he has no alternative strategy. The way out of this self-generated predicament (my rule for others is working against me) came by changing the rule about what other people 'should' and 'shouldn't' do. Any rule that is created for the benefit of others needs to be shared with those other people so they can have a say in defining it. In this case, as in so many, the rule only existed in Tom's head so no one even knew he was using it to assess their behaviour.

So, rules can be limiting or liberating. They can also be hard or soft and for the self or others. Generally, the harder the rule, the more limiting it will be. Softness allows rules to be updated, discarded or changed, depending on your experience. When you have rules for others who don't share your rules, prepare for a stressful time.

If this section has challenged you to scrutinise your rules and check which ones may not be in your best interest, then that was our purpose. Remember also that, once a set of rules is established, your unconscious mind takes over in applying them. You may not even be aware that others are judging your rules and forming opinions about you and the limitations you place on yourself. It makes sense, then, to give your route map a spring clean now and again.

The world offers a multitude of experiences and is constantly changing. People, technology and the environment never stand still for a moment. One day you may believe that you have everything worked out and the next it has changed again. It's not just technology that is changing either – people are changing the way they think. In the last 15 years, there has been a boom in personal development, coaching and self-help. Such rapid growth has been in response to people knowing that there is more out there, more to know, more to do, more to get involved with and, above all, more potential to fulfil.

Remember the kaleidoscope? It shows exactly the same pattern each time if left unturned, yet it has the potential to show thousands of variations with just the slightest twist. Take control of your kaleidoscope and create patterns that serve you well. After all, reality is what you shape it to be or, more accurately, *your* reality is what you shape it to be.

> your reality is what you shape it to be

The next chapter gives you some of the central rules or beliefs on which NLP is based. We like to think of them more as guides than beliefs, helping us to understand any interaction more intelligently than we might if we were to be judging our experience from a set of hard and fast rules.

brilliant tip

The next time you catch yourself starting to do something as a result of feeling or thinking any of the following:

- that you simply 'should' be doing it
- that 'others expect it of me'
- that 'I always do this'
- that 'everyone else is doing it'
- that 'others might think I'm odd if I don't'
- that 'this is what people should do'

and you would prefer not to, ask yourself these questions:

- 'Deep inside do I really want to be doing this?'
- 'What would I be doing if the rules above didn't apply to me?'
- 'So, what's stopping me?'
- 'What's the worst that could possibly happen if I did something different?'
- 'Is my rule for others causing me frustration?'

brilliant recap

In this chapter you have learned that:

● your communication has three key stages: taking in information through your senses; assimilating and processing information; communicating your results to others

● people make up rules which help the decision-making process; some rules work well, others act as limitations

● your rules affect each category of relationship, i.e. with other people, with your work and with yourself

● people have rules for all aspects of their lives; even if you decided not to have any rules, this would be a rule

● the important questions anyone can ask themselves are, 'Are my rules working for me?', 'Do my rules help me to enjoy life?', 'Which of my rules are redundant or in need of an upgrade?'

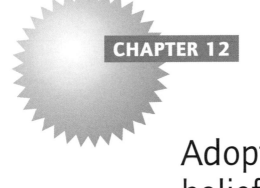

CHAPTER 12

Adopting the beliefs on which NLP is based

Now that you have some experience of NLP, adopting the beliefs on which it is founded will expedite your journey to success. NLP was originally used to model excellence. The following beliefs were modelled from people who excelled in their field. They are referred to as the 'presuppositions' of NLP.

The map is not the territory

You have your own unique understanding of the world around you. Whatever your perception is, it isn't how it *actually* is! You can never have *all* the information *all* the time. Just as a map doesn't show every house, shop, tree or bump in the road, your map is merely your representation of the world rather than reality.

brilliant example

Sue and Sam went shopping at the same supermarket at the same time.

Sam would shop intuitively, without a list, but, for Sue, shopping was like a military campaign. She took a list of what she needed, worked out an efficient route through the aisles and bought only what was on the list.

Sue could never quite understand how Sam would wander around the supermarket aimlessly, choosing items he fancied, while Sam would make fun of Sue's regimented precision.

You create your map by filtering information through your senses, the language you use, your beliefs and values and your experience.

Respect others' maps of the world

Developing a state of curiosity is one of the most useful things you can do if you are going to communicate successfully. If everyone's map is different, who is to say who has the right one or the best one? An effective state of curiosity will allow you to gain information about the other person's map, which will help you to build rapport, as well as communicate with and influence him or her. An effective state of curiosity includes a healthy respect for other people's maps. It does not mean that you have to agree, but it is useful to understand them.

▶ brilliant example

Ingrid's map differed from her son Greg's.

His mother was away for the weekend, so Greg decided to invite his friends round for a party. Things got out of hand and considerable damage was caused.

Greg was very apologetic, thus respecting Ingrid's map, and Ingrid respected Greg's desire to have teenage fun. Together they were able to work out a plan to get the house put right.

The meaning of your communication is in the response you get

Taking responsibility for your communication will give you control over the process and the results. It is common for people to give their view of something and then blame others or circumstances when they are not understood.

If you want control over your success, then take responsibility for your communication. If you don't get the response you expected first time, then try explaining things differently.

> if you want control over your success, then take responsibility for your communication

🔘 brilliant example

Harry was passionate about his new idea and used all the expressive body language he could muster to explain it to Tara. Tara sat, hardly moving, as she listened intently. Harry interpreted this as 'Tara is not interested'.

If it's possible for one person, it's possible for others

You have all the resources you need to make changes in your life. In situations where you find yourself struggling to achieve, it's not that you don't have the internal resources, it's just that you are in an unresourceful state.

> you have all the resources you need to make changes in your life

Developing resourceful states is crucial to the pursuit of success. You can achieve anything you decide, but some things will take longer than others. Be sure to check the consequences of dedicating your life to achieving your aspirations.

🔘 brilliant example

Years ago, doctors believed that if you ran fast enough to complete a mile within four minutes your heart would stop – until Roger Bannister did it. No sooner had Roger achieved the four-minute mile than his record was broken over and over again by other athletes whose beliefs had changed.

There is no failure, only feedback

If what you do isn't creating the desired result, you have still created *a* result. Use the feedback you receive to explore what you can do differently to get the outcome you want. Ask yourself, 'What can I learn from this?' and 'What can I do differently?'

focus on solutions not on problems

Focus on solutions and what else is possible, not on problems. Failure exists only as a state of mind – a perception.

brilliant example

Charles gave a presentation on a project that went off the rails. Rather than talking about failure and looking for someone to blame, he focused instead on what had been learned, and how that learning was going to be used to exercise more control over future projects.

Mind and body are part of the same system

The way you think has a direct impact on your physiology. If your thoughts are making you feel sad, then your body will reflect this. If your thoughts are making you feel happy, then your body will reflect this, too. Negative thinking has a tendency to cause stress and tension, blocking energy flow. Indeed, it is increasingly recognised that serious illnesses can be caused by the build-up of stress. Clearly, it makes sense to keep energy flowing by thinking positively.

brilliant example

Watch any sportsmen and women at the top of their game and you will see how they think their way to success. They do it by generating a positive belief and state of control followed by consistent practice.

Every behaviour has a positive intention

You make the best choices you can with the resources you have available at the time. The intention relating to your choice is a positive one for you, even though others may not see it that way.

brilliant example

Ben chose not to telephone a girl he met at a party the previous evening, even though they got on really well and she had been delighted when he asked for her telephone number. Past experience of relationships with girls told Ben that he would get hurt. His behaviour reflected his positive intention to protect himself from perceived future hurt, but the girl was disappointed when he didn't call.

The person with the most flexibility will control the system

Flexibility in relation to thinking and behaviour will give you the advantage when it comes to understanding other people's maps of reality, building rapport and achieving outcomes. Being too fixed and rigid can create a stalemate situation, with no desired outcomes being achieved, and can also restrict the number of people with whom you can build rapport.

Flexibility does not mean giving way to every idea, but, rather, being able to adapt, pace and lead with your thinking and behaviour. Inflexibility is narrow-mindedness, having fixed ideas and 'one way of doing things'.

brilliant example

Janine wondered why she hadn't been promoted. She had been with her company in the same role for a number of years and had watched people come into the organisation and go on to receive promotion before her.

Janine did her job well but hadn't realised that she 'chose' who to associate with on the basis of those she got on well with and inadvertently alienated everyone else.

Promotion came easily once she learned to flex her behaviour to achieve her well-formed outcomes.

If you always do what you've always done, you'll always get what you've always had

> until you reprogramme your thinking, your results are unlikely to change

Unconscious programming causes you to repeat patterns, even though you are aware that they are not working. Until you reprogramme your thinking, your results are unlikely to change.

brilliant example

Brian had been married three times and had had a number of other unsuccessful relationships.

He blamed the women in his life for his inability to make the relationships last. Unfortunately, he approached every relationship in the same way, making no changes to his thinking and behaviour, but expecting his partners to make changes to accommodate him. Once he became aware that he did this, he was able to make changes that involved respecting his partner's map.

Your behaviour is not who you are

Behaviour is something you do that is given meaning by other people. In other words, people make their own interpretations of your behaviour by using their own maps. Chances are, their interpretations are often inaccurate. Successful people remember to look beyond behaviour in their interactions with others.

> successful people remember to look beyond behaviour in their interactions

brilliant example

Thomas had spent a number of years in the Navy.

He had lied about his age and was accepted before he was 16. He had to harden up quickly and took a lot of abuse from his contemporaries. Consequently, he shaved his head, wore an earring and underwent weight training.

When Thomas eventually left the Navy, he still had the strong-man appearance he had needed in the service for his own protection. Underneath, though, he was a passionate, creative man with some exceptional ideas for business.

Your perception is your reality

Your map of reality is created by the way you perceive things. Your perception of a situation will be different from that of, say, your next-door neighbour or your partner, offspring, manager or colleague.

On the basis that no two people can possibly have exactly the same experience, there are very few universal truths.

brilliant example

Rob became irritated because his girlfriend was consistently late for dates. He felt that she didn't love and respect him and he became angry whenever they were together.

Fiona didn't place such a high value on time as Rob and found it hard to stick to a timetable. Her meetings with Rob were becoming increasingly unpleasant as he was invariably in a bad temper. She confided to her friend that she wanted to finish the relationship and find someone who was more fun to be with.

You are in charge of your mind and, therefore, your results

Everything starts with one thought. If you are in control of your thoughts, you are in control of your behaviour and, therefore, your results.

brilliant example

Talking to Hannah the other day, it became clear that she was limiting her results with her narrow way of thinking. She consistently used language such as, 'I can't see that ever happening', 'It would be all right if only ...', 'They [the management] will never allow that to happen'.

Spending her time thinking about what *wasn't* possible was leaving Hannah bereft when it came to finding solutions.

Resistance is a sign of a lack of rapport

After you have taken the trouble to build rapport with someone, you can lead and pace them to a win–win outcome. When rapport is absent, there will be signs of resistance – he or she will carry on with an activity while you are talking or there will be mismatches in your body postures. Without rapport, win–win outcomes are unlikely to be achieved.

brilliant example

Liam doesn't like 'small talk'. He is a young man bursting with ideas, but lacks the finesse to get them across.

We taught Liam that 'small talk' is actually 'very big talk'. Without rapport, communication becomes strained and then ideas are often never aired.

You cannot *not* communicate

In the 1960s, Professor Albert Mehrabian conducted some research into the effectiveness of spoken communication. It resulted in the following statistics:

- 7 per cent of meaning is in the words that are spoken
- 38 per cent of meaning is in the way the words are said
- 55 per cent of meaning is in body language and facial expression.

Although these statistics are approximate – and are distorted when the telephone is being used – they highlight the importance of facial expression, body language and tone

> whatever you do ... someone will be attaching meaning to your behaviour

of voice in the communication process. Whatever you do, even if you think you are sitting quietly minding your own business, someone will be attaching meaning to your behaviour.

brilliant example

Farhat had decided that, to get on in business, you had to hold back
your emotions and not give anything away with your body language. On
a training seminar, Mathew, one of the other participants, stayed until
everyone else had left to tell us, 'I don't know what it is about Farhat, but
I wouldn't trust her one little bit.' It is easy to pick up the signals from a
person who knowingly attempts to suppress their emotions. You pick up
the lack of expression. Even when you think you are not communicating
anything, others are interpreting your body language and attitude from
what is missing. Mathew was picking up something from Farhat, but,
unsure what it was, he just felt uneasy with her in the same room. There is
a well-known saying, 'Attitudes are infectious, is yours worth catching?'

You have all the resources you need to change

Believing this will help you to help yourself and others find the
resources you need to make changes that serve you well.

brilliant example

Debbie revealed to us that she didn't have a very long attention span.

It transpired that she had been told this by a well-meaning geography
teacher at school who really meant, 'You are not paying attention at this
moment to the subject I am teaching you.' Debbie, though, had carried this
with her ever since, believing that she couldn't sit still in a whole variety of
scenarios.

When we pointed out that Debbie *could* sit very still, focus when watching
a film and for long periods when reading books by her favourite author,
it was a simple process to draw out the resources she already had in one
situation and apply them to another.

There is learning in everything that happens

Whether we perceive something to be a mistake or otherwise, there is always some learning to be gleaned from everything we do and everything that happens.

---

brilliant example

When Niall Fitzgerald was being tipped as successor to the CEO of Unilever, someone recalled how he had been involved in the now famous Persil Power episode (ranked number 7 out of 100 brand failures in *Brand Failures* by author Matt Haig, Kogan Page, 2005).

Persil Power had been an attempt in 1994 by Unilever to break the stalemate in the soap powder wars by launching a new product credited with vastly superior performance.

Unfortunately for Unilever, arch rivals Procter & Gamble learned that repeated use of the new powder seemed to cause rotting of some fabrics. This message was conveyed quickly to the public and Persil Power's fate was sealed. Unilever had to admit a £350m mistake and public humiliation.

When a journalist asked how the man who was responsible for that mistake could possibly be promoted to the top slot, the answer came back that, as Unilever had spent £350m educating him, it had no choice but to make him CEO.

Problems only exist in your head

Outside your head, there are only circumstances, so, whether you see things as a problem or not depends entirely on your perspective, which comes from your personal map of the world. As Albert Einstein said, 'You can't solve a problem with the same thinking that created it.'

If you want to understand, do something

The best way to understand anything is to take action, get involved, and have an experience about which you can form a considered view. All the reading and listening in the world is no substitute for personal experience.

brilliant tip

In order to test your alignment with the underlying principles of NLP, ask yourself these two questions regarding each one:

● What would happen if I lived by this principle?

● What would happen if I lived by the opposite of this principle?

brilliant recap

In this chapter you have learned that:

● every person creates their own unique map of the world

● being curious, respectful and non-judgemental about others' maps is the first step to influencing them

● NLP is based upon a set of presuppositions (beliefs that have no truth of their own) and, when you act as if they are true, then NLP can work magic for you

● by living more fully within the presuppositions, you can avoid the traps other people set for themselves with beliefs that hinder progress and act as limitations.

CHAPTER 13

Extra NLP techniques

T his chapter offers a compendium of additional techniques not already mentioned in the body of this book. Where you would use each one is described at the beginning of each technique.

Perceptual positions

Use this technique to understand other people's maps of reality and reach mutually beneficial agreements when, for example, preparing for meetings, dealing with family members – including children, handling customers, selling, negotiating, coaching and giving presentations.

When rapport is low and you are not getting along with someone you want to influence, it helps if you can see the relationship from the other person's point of view. The ability to look at an issue from a number of different perspectives can greatly add to the amount of information you have and help you to make better decisions and choices.

Seeing things from others' perspectives is a great start, but to hear and feel things from their perspectives as well is even more useful. By acting as if you are someone else, you can begin to understand some of their beliefs, values and representations and gain a more complete understanding of how they might behave and react to the things you say and do. It enables you to under-stand others more and expand your own level of awareness.

The following exercise is designed to help you gain a perspective on any given situation from three angles.

1   Think of a situation that you are going to face in the near future – one causing you some anxiety, frustration or apprehension.

2   You are going to view the situation from three different angles. Set a scene as though you are getting ready for a play, using props such as chairs and tables.

3   *First position – you* In this position, consider things only from your own point of view. You want to know how things affect you and how you feel. This first position is really useful when you want to assert yourself, check out how you feel about a situation or outcome and ensure that your needs are met. Staying here all the time, however, is unhelpful as you will have little, or no, awareness of your impact on others or their needs and preferences. You may also jump to conclusions without fully checking them out.

4   *Second position – the other person's shoes* Physically put yourself in the position of the other person in your scene. From here you can look back at yourself in the first position, step in to the other person's shoes and experience things the way they do. This is more than thinking about what you would do if you were them, it is about projecting 'you' into 'him or her' and really understanding the other person's perspective to gain more accurate information. What are his or her priorities? What pressure is he or she under? What values and beliefs are driving the person's behaviour? Adopting this position gives you a better understanding of the other person's behaviour and map of reality and, consequently, how he or she perceives you.

5   *Third position – fly on the wall* Now stand away from the scene so that you can see yourself in the first position and the other person in the second. From here, take on the role of

an independent observer, detached and dissociated from the other two positions. Imagine you are a film director or a fly-on-the-wall documentary producer. You are observing from a logical, rational and objective perspective. In this position you may notice what both parties can do differently to improve the relationship and achieve a win–win outcome.

6   Revisit any of the above positions to gain further understanding.

All three positions are equally valuable. By carrying out this exercise in real space and time, you can increase your under-standing, your chances of building better rapport, create new ideas and solutions and open up new ways of thinking.

The swish technique

Use this technique to change a habit – for example, biting your nails, picking at skin, clockwatching, poor performance in sport, road rage, eating habits (identify specific triggers such as comfort eating or excitement). You can also use it to change your response to something, such as from 'immediate' to 'considered' or 'aggressive' to 'assertive'.

1   Choose a past negative situation where you demonstrated the behaviour you want to change. Create a fully associated image in your mind. Focus on what happened. Put a frame around the image. Identify one or two qualities of your internal image that, when intensified, change your internal response – you will probably notice the change as a feeling. Usually the brightness and size work best, but colour, contrast, location or depth may work also. Play around with this until you are happy with the chosen qualities.

2   Change your state by taking some deep breaths and stretching.

3   Create an image in your mind of the behaviour you would like to have instead. Really see yourself doing it. Make your picture dissociated – you are looking at yourself in the picture. Dissociated pictures create the motivation for moving towards something you want. Include all the resources you will need – strength, confidence, clarity of thought, listening ability, creativity, focus, relaxation, humour. Make your image compelling and realistic and check it out with respect to other areas of your life. Try it out with different contexts – is this 'new you' ecological with other relationships? If you were to respond in this way in different contexts, would the outcome be favourable to you and those you interact with? You may want to alter the image so that you are completely happy with it. When you are, intensify it and make it really compelling.

4   Shrink the image down to the size of a postage stamp, allowing the colour to drain out of it and all the sounds to become dull and muted.

5   Change your state.

6   Take your first image and increase the two strongest qualities you chose in step 1. Next, take your new self-image that you have shrunk and put it in the bottom corner of your first image. The next step should be done quickly. Say to yourself

'swish' and, instantaneously, make the large picture small and dark, while making the new self-image large and bright. Make them swap places instantly and the negative image disappear completely.

Swish Technique

7 Repeat step 6 about five times, making sure that you change your state by taking some deep breaths and stretching between each one. Speed and repetition are essential.

8 Test your new response by imagining a time in the future when you will want this different response. This is called 'future pacing'. If you still get the original response, go back to step 1 and repeat the exercise. You will know when you have been successful because you will no longer be able to bring back the negative image.

New behaviour generator

Use this technique to create an entirely new behaviour.

1 With your eyes down to the left, ask yourself, 'If I were able to ... [state your goal], what would I look like?'

2 With eyes up to the right, construct a visual image of what you would look like if you were in the act of achieving your goal. Construct the image from a dissociated point of view.

3 Mentally step inside the image so that you now feel yourself doing what you just saw yourself doing in the image. What do you see, hear and feel?

4 Compare the feelings you have with the feelings from a similar experience in which you were successful.

5 If the two feelings match, then you have finished.

6 If the two feelings don't match, then name what is missing – creativity, more confidence, being more relaxed, and so on.

7 Refine your goal statement by adding 'and ... [name the additional resource(s) you have chosen]'.

8 Go back to step 1 and repeat the exercise.

Visual squash

Use this technique to resolve conflicting beliefs or values in yourself. The trigger here is generally when you hear yourself saying, 'Part of me wants to do/believes X and part of me wants to do/believes Y.'

1 Identify your conflicting beliefs or wants.

2 Create a visual representation of each part, one in each hand, and hold them out in front of you.

3 Identify an outcome and ask for agreement from both parts.

4   Ask each part for its positive intention and continue chunking up to higher-level values until you reach agreement.

5   Have each part look at the other and say what it sees and thinks. Include resources, strengths, beliefs and expectations.

6   Ask both parts to state their readiness to give and receive resources or negotiate if necessary.

7   Bring both hands together and pull both parts inside you to integrate them within you. They should do so willingly.

8   Check for objections from any other parts. If there are any objections, then do the exercise again with the objecting part present. Put this new part on a chair where you can relate to it from a distance.

Focus

If you find that, when doing certain activities, you are easily distracted, this technique will be very useful.

You will find that in some circumstances you are able to focus very well. It may be when you are watching a favourite television programme, shopping, enjoying a night out with friends, cutting your fingernails, shaving, combing your hair or reading a book you really enjoy. It's important to recognise that it is not 'all the time' you are unable to focus, which means you can spread this ability to other activities.

So, having identified an activity where you tend to lose focus and are easily distracted, ask yourself if it is of any value to you. What do you get from it? If you chose not to do it, what would the consequences be? Connecting with the outcome of any task will help you to engage fully with it; you will have a stronger purpose for doing it and doing it well.

Even when you are clear about the outcome of a task, however, and can see positive benefits for getting it done, the act of doing it may present a hurdle for you. It may be that, when you think of doing the task, you lose heart in it and lack the motivation to get started. If only you could get started. If you force yourself while being reluctant, though, you have forces working against you. Part of you wants to have the benefit that comes with completion and the other wishes you didn't have to do the task at all. When you approach anything in such a frame of mind, and state, you have set yourself up to be easily distracted.

So, here's what you do. Recognise the feeling of avoidance. Where is the emotional tug coming from? Tell yourself that your state of avoidance is not serving you well and you really do want the benefit that comes from having done the task. Visualise having completed the task. Turn up the brightness, contrast and colour. Make sure you are projecting your mental image of having completed the task above the horizon level, intensify the image qualities even further and notice the feeling of satisfaction you have created.

Now, keep hold of that feeling and relax your breathing. Let go of any tension around your eyes, jaw and shoulders and gaze into the palm of your hand. Tell yourself that you are going to focus so much that wild horses will not be able to distract you – and neither will any other external sound, ringing phone, new e-mail, door closing, children shouting or traffic driving by. As you look into your palm, observe the detail on the surface of the skin. Look into the smallest crease and see how the lines join. Then look below the surface of the skin at the different colours – shades of red, yellow, blue. How many different shades of colour can you notice? After doing this for one minute, your attention will be highly focused. So now, keeping the same state of mind and with a clear, positive intention to do a job well, move your focus from your hand to the task before you and get on with it!

Image mapping

This technique is very fast and can be used to transfer internal resources, such as confidence, patience, humour, focus and decisiveness, from one context to another. It uses internal imagery – a little like the swish technique but more subtle – to give you new options in situations where you have been experiencing difficulty. Use this technique when you may want to use a particular resource in more than one situation.

It is surprising how precise your mental imagery is in relation to your state of mind. So, for example, whenever you are feeling a certain way – perhaps anxious or frustrated – you will recreate the exact same imagery, internal dialogue and feelings that have become habitual in certain situations. So precise will this habit be that your mental imagery will always be in the same location, the same size, brightness and contrast as well as colour or black and white. You can test this by catching yourself in any mood and noticing your mental imagery. Do the same the next time you are in the same mood and check – your imagery will be identical. We can use this knowledge to create a lasting state change.

Habits are so powerful. The moment you have received a communication from someone, you will be firing a habitual response – click, click, click. There is little time to check what you are doing and make an alternative choice. Habits are hard-wired in. This technique allows you to choose to revisit one of those moments and, instead of responding in the usual way, remain resourceful and poised.

This is how you do it.

1   Recall a time when you reacted negatively to a person or situation.

2   Pay attention to the following aspects of your internal imagery:

   ● Location – where are you projecting this image precisely?

   ● Size – what shape is it and what size?

   ● Is it colour or black and white?

   ● Is there any sound with this image? If so, describe the audio qualities.

   ● How clear is the image? How bright is it?

3   Now, break this state by taking a very deep breath and adjusting your posture.

4   Decide what state you would like to replace the habitual one with. Let's call it state X.

5   Recall a situation when you had a strong experience of being in state X. The strength or intensity of the state is important. Make sure you choose a powerful state, not a weak one.

6   Pay attention to the aspects of your internal imagery described in step 2 that are attached to the experience.

7   Now, retrieve your first image and move it so that it maps over the second more resourceful image associated with state X. The picture will remain the same, but take on the aspects of image X.

Job done. Now, try to get back the first image in its original location and you will find that it doesn't want to appear there any more. It will automatically shift to the new location with the new aspects and you will feel much more resourceful.

Image mapping can be used for many different states. I encourage you to play with it and explore the many resourceful states you can create for yourself for any context in which you want to feel more in control.

The wall of concentration

This is a very useful technique to enable you to maintain your concentration in a noisy environment. We have taught this technique to children who find it difficult to concentrate on their work because of the noise level in their classrooms.

1 Imagine that you have a soundproof frosted glass wall around you. Everything is still happening around you, but the sound is muted and you can only see hazy images through the glass.

2 You can develop the technique further by:

● imagining yourself pulling the glass up and down as and when you need it

● creating a noticeboard on the glass, on which you can place sticky notes to remind yourself of things to do later

● installing a thermostat so that you can control the temperature while you are concentrating.

Once you know how your mind works, there are infinite possibilities for making this technique work positively for you.

Inner dialogue control

What exactly do you say to yourself when the inner dialogue – or should we say monologue – cuts in? What we say to ourselves can easily become repetitive and habitual and turn into a monologue of instructions. It's a good idea, then, to make sure that our internal conversations are positive and useful rather than downbeat and not very useful.

So, let's look at the three main relationships most of us have – with our work and activities, other people and ourselves. As you think about each of these areas in turn, take a negative example from each – something you don't particularly like about yourself, a task you dread doing and someone you have been procrastinating about telephoning.

Notice the tone in which you talk to yourself about each of the examples, notice the speed and inflection of your internal voice and be aware of the location of the voice, too. Is it coming from the left, right, in front of you, behind you or from somewhere else?

Now do the same with a positive example from each area – something you particularly enjoy doing, someone whose company you enjoy and something you really like about yourself. Notice the difference in the tone, speed and pitch of your internal voice and the direction from which it comes. It is more than likely very different from the way you talked to yourself in the negative examples.

Once you are aware of the dialogue you have with yourself, if you decide that it isn't useful, you can play with it to reduce the negativity. Try some of these ideas:

● Imagine that you have a volume control – turn it down so that you can no longer hear it.

● Look up – it's almost impossible to talk to yourself with your eyes looking in this direction.

● Turn the voice into a cartoon character.

● Turn up the speed so that it sounds like a chipmunk.

● Turn down the speed so that it sounds very deep and ridiculous.

Power up your inner dialogue

Give your inner voice an emotional characteristic, so, for example, if you have a goal you want to achieve, then create a statement such as, 'I am going to achieve my goal through persistence, commitment and determination'. Put an emotional emphasis on each of the words so that you actually feel it when you say them. Feel free to exaggerate your voice, like an actor overplaying a part – after all, it's only in your head so no one else is going to hear it, but they will see the difference it makes to your attitude and energy on the outside. You can be creative with this technique by imagining a variety of voices, arranged all around your head, all saying your goal statement together. The best way to use this is to have fun with it.

Bring it on!

This technique is a variation on the swish technique and works well when you can easily visualise scenarios. If you are not great at visualising, however, we recommend practising it so that you *can* use this and other powerful visualising techniques.

Use this technique when you want to do something but are holding yourself back. It could be that you are imagining ways in which an event will be difficult or problematic or you are attaching fear and creating anxiety for yourself. Maybe you want to make a good impression somewhere, at a job interview or customer meeting, or maybe with your board of directors. It could be a first date or a bungee jump. This technique will change your state from one of fear, trepidation and uncertainty to one where every cell in your body is pulsating with enthusiasm and excitement and shouting … 'Bring it on!'

This technique can dramatically change both the internal representation and feelings associated with your future event in such a way that wild horses will not be able to hold you back. What you are going to do is take all your negative images, sounds and feelings and dissolve them with powerful positive representations so that you are able to act convincingly and proactively, being fully engaged in the event.

1   Bring to mind the event ahead of you. Run through the
    following questions in your mind. Take one at a time and
    see your answers as lifelike images. Resist any desire to write
    down your answers – you need to be fully associated with the
    experience in your mind in order to generate answers that have
    deep meaning for you.

    ● Why are you even contemplating this?

    ● Do you have a choice as to whether you go ahead with this
      or not?

    ● If you choose not to, how will you feel afterwards?

    ● If you go ahead and succeed, how will you feel afterwards?

    ● Is there any practical reason for not going ahead?

    If, after answering the questions above, you still want to
    proceed, continue with the exercise.

2   Imagine that you have completed the event triumphantly.
    Answer the following questions, using the same process as
    before and bringing the answers to life in your imagination:

    ● How does it feel to have succeeded?

    ● What does this success mean to you?

    ● How are things different for you and your relationships
      now?

    ● As you look to the horizon, what else is possible?

    Next, build a gallery of images. Begin by taking each of the
    above answers and work on the image you have connected with
    it. Make the image dissociated by putting a frame around it.
    Make it large and close up. Turn up the colour, brightness and
    contrast. See yourself in the image and notice the location of
    the image in your internal visual field. Do this for each image
    connected with your answers to the four questions above.
    Position the images in your visual field so that they wrap
    around and encompass you. You now have a wall of highly

motivating images all around you. Make sure that they are all
bright and colourful.

3   Add sound to your gallery of images. Start a rhythm going in
    your mind and spread it around your body. This is an intuitive
    process. Create the rhythm first and a piece of music will
    emerge to fit the rhythm you have generated. When you have
    the music, turn up the volume, adjust the treble, middle and
    bass to improve the quality and make it surround sound. Bring
    this whole audiovisual inner experience into your mind five
    or six times so that it burns into your imagination. The more
    you focus on it, the more motivated and enthusiastic you will
    become.

Now, how do you feel about the event?

Bring it on!

New directions

This technique is useful if you feel that you are at a dead end or
junction in your life or career and want to move in a new direction, but are uncertain which one to take. Often a number of
options seem appealing, but choosing can be stressful, especially
if you have an options metaprogramme. It will be even more
daunting if you also have a considering metaprogramme. What
if you choose the wrong one? What if all the choices are equally
appealing to you? What if you have an away from metaprogramme and have been making choices using criteria to decide
what you don't want? Deciding what you do want can be very
puzzling and confusing.

We designed this exercise to help people overcome their natural
reactions to change, be more decisive and associate positively
with the direction they would like to go in next. There is often

a tendency to use an intellectual process to make decisions like this, writing everything down on paper, a process that dissociates you from your emotions. This exercise, instead, allows you to really experience, through your feelings, what your new direction might be like. This is important if you want to enjoy your new direction.

People perform well at jobs they enjoy and poorly at jobs they dislike. This exercise is the next best thing to the real experience and gives you the opportunity to check out three, four or even more possible future directions.

It is best done with someone who can guide you through it as it requires you to be fully associated with imaginary scenarios. This exercise is similar to the new behaviour generator except that, rather than creating a new behaviour, you create a number of reference experiences. You use these to make comparisons and then choose the strongest, most fulfilling, enjoyable and motivating direction.

1   Brainstorm to come up with a list of possible new directions. There is no upper limit to the number of options, although, clearly, the longer the list, the longer the exercise will take.

2   You will need a large space and will need to pick a time when you can do the exercise without interruptions. Allow around 1 square metre (11 square feet) per option. For each of your options, draw a simple image or symbol to represent it on a sheet of A4 paper or card. When you have done this for each option, place them all on the floor, spacing them out as much as you can.

3   To help you with the next stage, we will work through an example. Let's say that one of the directions you want to take is to become a coach. Stand on the spot where you have placed the coach image. Fully associate with the experience of what it might be like. Close your eyes if it helps. Concentrate on

visualising the experience of being a coach. If you have a guide, he or she will take you through the following process, which is purposely written in the present tense. Make sure that you take time to process each directive using both your visual and auditory senses to create strong feelings.

● Imagine being a coach.

● Imagine finding your customers – how are you doing this?

● Imagine marketing your services.

● Imagine making a sale.

● Imagine a telephone call with someone wanting to make an appointment. You are meeting an executive and going through the process of coaching him or her.

● Imagine the next day, doing the same things with different clients.

● Imagine attending to the administration of running your business.

● Imagine the travelling.

How does this feel now? Rate the intensity of your feelings about this new direction from 0 to 10 (where 0 = low and 10 = high). Move on to the next possible new direction.

4 When you have completed this process for all your options, stand at a distance from the space you have used and look at each one in turn. Which one seems to stand out as the most enjoyable?

Has this helped you to decide? We wish you every success with your new direction.

Becoming an optimist

One of the areas of difference between people is the degree of optimism or pessimism in their thinking process. When pessimism is greater than optimism, the labels sceptic, cynic or 'glass half empty' are often used. These labels generally describe a person who sees the negative in things and expects the worst to happen. The problem is that you usually get what you expect and it takes an awful lot of energy to think negatively. It has a knock-on effect on your overall health and well-being, too.

So, if you know you are a pessimist, how do you change into an optimist? First of all, you must want to make the change. You must want to change your dark, murky images into bright, colourful pictures; your negative self-talk into upbeat, rhythmic, positive messages. You must *want* to feel more energised and motivated.

Having switched on this state of desire, you are now in a position to bring about a permanent change. Any number of the techniques in this book will do the trick and here is another very quick one.

First, though, a quick reminder of the telltale signs of pessimism. Your internal images will most likely be fuzzy or even black and white, projected below the horizon level and often down on the ground. If you have been a pessimist for some time, your body posture may involve you bending forward to allow you access to your images in this location. Your internal dialogue is likely to be in full flow, with a dull tone and negatively orientated content. A good deal of your time may be spent inside your head, paying little attention to the world around you.

To become optimistic, you just reverse the process and add a little more into the mix. Practise the following every day until it becomes a habit.

1   Raise your head when you are walking and look around, paying
     attention to what you notice. Keep your eyes focused above the
     horizon level. Resist the urge to turn your attention inwards on
     your thoughts and feelings.

2   Raise the corner of your lips to make a cheeky little smile and
     take a few deep breaths. If you can find nothing to smile about,
     then smile about nothing - you don't need a reason to smile.

3   Slowly and gently nod your head up and down, as if affirming
     'yes' to nothing in particular. You can say 'yes' to just being
     alive.

4   Place the tip of your tongue on the roof of your mouth. This will
     reduce any tendency you have to talk to yourself.

5   Do all the above steps together and check how you feel. If you
     try to feel negative while you are doing these things you will
     find it is not so easy to do.

If you are following these steps, but telling yourself it's a load
of baloney, guess what – it's still going to work if you practise it
enough!

The more you practise this, the more optimistic you will become
and the easier you will find life in general. It will take a lot of
effort to be pessimistic about anything and, at a fundamental
level, what you are now saying to your pessimism with your mind
and body is 'no'. So, by reversing your physiology, the natural
result is to affirm 'yes', which takes far less energy.

If you want just one reason for switching from pessimism to
optimism this may be it:

*Optimists live longer, healthier lives than pessimists. Optimists have
fewer health problems and generally fewer problems in life. They have
30 per cent less chance of dying from heart disease than pessimists
and they also recover from illness more readily.*

To check the source of these statistics, visit the Mayo Clinic's website (**www.mayoclinic.com**). The clinic, in Rochester, Minnesota, has carried out extensive research on this topic.

Slowing down

Some people think and speak extremely fast, often leaving other people behind. When nervous, the speed can become out of control. There is a very simple technique you can use to slow yourself down. As you speak, hold your hands in front of you and rotate them in a backwards direction. It should look like you are turning a wheel backwards with your hands. Your speech will slow down to the speed at which your hands are turning, so, if you need to be even slower, just slow down your hands, and do the opposite direction if you want to speed up.

There is a less obvious version of this you can use if it is inappropriate to be seen turning invisible wheels. Imagine you have a waterwheel in front of you that fits snuggly into the curve of your neck underneath your chin. Imagine this waterwheel turning backwards as you speak and you will slow down just the same as if you were turning a wheel with your hands.

Pulling the plug on negative emotions

Some people get carried away by their emotions and find it difficult to perform well whilst in this condition. This technique can be used to take the energy away from the emotion forever. Most times when people want to avoid negative emotions they do things to distract themselves. The problem with this is that the emotion will keep coming back. The only way to resolve this is by facing the emotion and engaging with it so there are no further surprises that the emotion can demobilise you with. Read the following procedure, memorise it, and carry it out without interruption. You need to be somewhere quiet where you will not be disturbed. Here's what to do:

1   Recall the feeling and relax your shoulders. Breathe slowly from your lower abdomen as you close your eyes and focus your attention on the feeling.

2   Tell the feeling that it may have been useful in the past, but it no longer serves any purpose and that you are going to pull the plug and cut off its energy supply.

3   Move your attention slowly down inside the feeling until you find the very core and, as you come through the core and out the other side, imagine pulling a power cord.

4   As you pull the power cord, feel the energy in the emotion leave you. Imagine the energy leaving with each outward breath.

5   Draw in a new positive emotional energy as you inhale. You might give it a colour or form. It could be a symbol or other metaphor which comes to mind. Have this positive feeling fill you up and replace the vacuum left by the old feeling you no longer need.

6   Check how you feel.

brilliant tip

Once you have mastered a number of NLP techniques, be creative with them. You can mix and match techniques for maximum impact. For example, while running a perceptual positions exercise, described at the beginning of this chapter, you could introduce a visualisation, a belief change, even a swish or a visual squash (earlier in this chapter).

What next?

NLP is a skill that requires practice, and your journey through this book is the first step towards a better life using what you have learned. We trust that you have enjoyed it and encourage you to continue practising the techniques you found most useful on a daily basis. As a result of practice, you develop confidence and, over time, new ways of thinking and behaving will come to you naturally.

Remember, being stuck with programmes that are limiting you is your choice. NLP gives you tools that make it easy for you to exercise more choice about the way you experience life. Choose well.

How to contact the authors

David Molden: david@quadrant1.com

Pat Hutchinson: pat@quadrant1.com

Website: **www.quadrant1.com**
         www.BrilliantNLP.co.uk

? brilliant questions and answers

Q Is all NLP training the same?

A The core skills of NLP are taught on most NLP courses. Beyond those core skills, the application of them tends to be split between those wanting to use NLP in their role as therapists and counsellors and those wanting to use NLP for themselves in business. NLP lends itself to both very effectively. Some courses run for 20 days over a period of 6 months, while others condense the learning into one block of around 7 to 9 days. Some courses attract large numbers of people; others restrict their participants to smaller group sizes of between 6 and 24 and offer a higher level of support and facilitation. There is no one standard, just many different formats.

Q What does an NLP qualification do for me?

A The value of NLP is not in the qualification, but in using it. We know lots of people who call themselves practitioners because they have attended a course and received a certificate. Not all practitioners, however, have integrated the skills that they have learned. It depends how they have been taught. True practitioners don't need to tell you that they have a certificate as they demonstrate their skills by achieving well-formed outcomes elegantly and ecologically. A certificate only shows that someone has attended a course – nothing more.

Q How do I apply NLP to my everyday life?

A Take it one step at a time. When you feel a tug, describe what was happening, without making a judgement. Avoid saying, 'He made me feel bad' or 'They won't listen to me'. Just describe what you noticed, such as, 'He put on a face and I felt uncertain and anxious'. Then refer to the book and decide which technique to use for that specific experience. Keep using it and it will become easier.

Q What is the best way to learn NLP?

A Our advice is to learn in a small group where you will receive expert tuition. During the learning process, many small nuances may be missed as two learners take turns playing the explorer and the facilitator. Access to experienced trainers at this stage is key if learners are to maximise their potential. From then on, it's practice, practice and more practice.

Take one aspect, such as eye-position cues, and spend a whole week noticing how people move their eyes and what that suggests about how they are thinking (not *what* they are thinking – that would be an interpretation). The next week, practise matching and mirroring body language, then, the week after that, listen to voice tone, and so on. After a while, you will begin to do these things automatically. The more you practise, the easier it will become.

Q I get the impression that NLP is like an exclusive club. I meet people who speak NLP jargon that I don't understand. Can you explain it?

A Such people are not demonstrating their skills – they are showing off. Good practitioners make you feel comfortable in their company and show a genuine interest in you without talking in jargon.

Q I have heard that NLP is manipulative. Is that true?

A A knife can be used to manipulate someone to hand over all his or her valuables. It can also be used to manipulate a stone from a cherry. Like any tool or weapon, it's the intention of the person using it that's important. If something can be used to manipulate, does that mean we must view it negatively? What about the knives and forks in your kitchen? Act on what you know, not on what you hear people say.

Q I have heard that there is no scientific evidence for NLP. Is that true?

A NLP has pulled together the works of a number of eminent therapists, researchers and linguists. Dr Richard Bandler and Dr John Grinder studied the works of Alfred Korzybski, Milton Erickson, Virginia Satir and Fritz

Pearls, to name but a few, and were encouraged by Gregory Bateson. Just Google these names if you want to trace the roots of NLP and read the early books by Bandler and Grinder.

NLP is eclectic. It draws from many disciplines that have their models and techniques grounded in both science and empirical evidence (see *Roots of Neurolinguistic Programming* by Robert Dilts, Metamorphous Press, 1989). Of course, like anything new, there are always people who feel threatened by NLP and seek to put it down in favour of their own pet theories. Remember that Galileo was imprisoned for showing evidence that the Earth revolved around the Sun. It took over a generation before his theory was accepted by the majority. The only real way to find out if NLP works is to try it for yourself.

Index